dying well

By definition, death lies beyond ⟨ moderns, it is an uncomfortable subject, the skeleton in every person's cupboard'. It is therefore the more valuable to have the opportunity to explore what lies a⟨... ⟩ almo⟨...⟩ knowledgeable and ⟨ ⟩ art ⟨ ⟩

Professor Wyatt ⟨...⟩ nger ⟨...⟩ ath ⟨...⟩ in his work as a neonatal consultant, he has daily ⟨...⟩ed, ⟨...⟩ and wrestled with what happens to human bodies towards the end of life – and not just to the body but also to the whole person. He has written, lectured and mentored on many aspects of the subject, and approaches it from a totally biblical world-view, making accessible what Christian revelation has to teach us. He draws on much that has been written, as well as on moving testimonies from those aware that death was imminent. He also draws from their relatives, friends, physicians and carers.

As a helpful framework, he borrows from the long-past Christian tradition of *ars moriendi* – the art of dying – discerning behind the medieval mindset centuries of wisdom, humanity and Christian devotion, as well as from detailed exposition from the example of Jesus himself, including the Seven Words from the cross.

The book, like its author, is in no doubt that death is unnatural to God's original purpose – 'the last enemy', as Paul describes it – and cannot finally prevail. Yet our Father has his purposes for each of us in our death and faithful dying, and it is never too soon to begin thinking about them. We could ask for no wiser or more honest, practical and compassionate guide.
Timothy Dudley-Smith, hymn writer

It is easy to shrink from the subjects of death and bereavement. Here, John Wyatt, an experienced physician, deals with the issues sensitively and clearly. Hidden fears are faced with comforting reassurances for those about to die and for their loved ones. The book deals with relevant physical, emotional and spiritual issues, as well as offering practical and legal advice. Timely chapters on how the Lord Jesus faced his death, and the joys of resurrection to follow, remind us that our grief need never be without hope. Whatever brings the reader into the final valley, here is light for the way and ease for the pain.
Janet Goodall, paediatrician and author

What a life-affirming book about dying this is. It had the curious and joyous impact of making me even more grateful for life, clearer about its preciousness and more eager to make the most of whatever

days God may grant me. The book's brilliance lies in the effortless way that John blends deep biblical insight, long experience of compassionately accompanying the old, middle-aged, young and very young through death, and world-class medical expertise with a clear-eyed cultural critique of the way over-medicalization has worked to strip dying of its potential to nourish spiritual growth, relational healing and enriching leave-taking. Full of careful, wise practical advice for the dying, and for all those involved, what emerges is a gentle, unsentimental, moving and liberating gift to us all.
Mark Greene, Executive Director, London Institute for Contemporary Christianity

John Wyatt writes with the heart of a pastor, the knowledge and skill of an experienced physician and the seasoned wisdom of a Christian believer who has walked the journey of grief himself. He offers a pathway to 'dying well' for us all, however trying the circumstances of death may prove to be. Biblical, practical and full of wise insight, this deeply helpful and relevant book is important whether death seems a distant reality or is staring us in the face. Much of the material has been warmly received in the context of the Keswick Convention and I am delighted now to be able to commend it to a wider audience.
John Risbridger, Minister and Team Leader, Above Bar Church, Southampton

A real treasure: encouraging, heart-warming, informative and sensible. It answers the concern of many Christian doctors that the will-o'-the-wisp of medical imperialism has led the Christian community astray into excessive medicalization of the process of dying, to the detriment of spiritual and family matters. John Wyatt writes very practically about dying with honesty and integrity. He shows us what can be learnt from Jesus' death and resurrection. He emphasizes the ultimate conquest of death, our 'mysterious and dreadful enemy'. This is a book for everyone that will change souls for the better.
Andrew Sims, former President of the Royal College of Psychiatrists and Emeritus Professor of Psychiatry of the University of Leeds

Drawing from our Christian past to help us face our future as Christians, *Dying Well* is wise, warm and refreshingly real.
Dan Strange, Oak Hill College

john wyatt

dying well

INTER-VARSITY PRESS
36 Causton Street, London SW1P 4ST, England
Email: ivp@ivpbooks.com
Website: www.ivpbooks.com

First published 2018

British Library Cataloguing-in-Publication Data
A catalogue record for this book is available from the British Library.

ISBN: 978–1–78359–485–6
eBook ISBN: 978–1–78359–486–3
Set in Dante 12/15 pt

Typeset in Great Britain by CRB Associates, Potterhanworth, Lincolnshire
Printed in Great Britain by Ashford Colour Press Ltd, Gosport, Hampshire

Inter-Varsity Press publishes Christian books that are true to the Bible and that communicate the gospel, develop discipleship and strengthen the church for its mission in the world.

IVP originated within the Inter-Varsity Fellowship, now the Universities and Colleges Christian Fellowship, a student movement connecting Christian Unions in universities and colleges throughout Great Britain, and a member movement of the International Fellowship of Evangelical Students. Website: www.uccf.org.uk. That historic association is maintained, and all senior IVP staff and committee members subscribe to the UCCF Basis of Faith.

Contents

Foreword

I've known Professor John Wyatt for over twenty years and I would describe him as a man who heads towards pain, not away from it. Indeed, I have a suspicion that in his childhood his parents may have lingered a little bit too long and intently on the horrifying sin of omission in the parable of the Good Samaritan, as the priest and the Levite passed by on the other side (see Luke 10:31–32)! Certainly, it seems to me, John never passes by on the other side and the result is that, at All Souls Church time and again over the years, he has made a profound difference to people's lives and deaths. With that in mind, I suppose I should have guessed that the theme of this book, *ars moriendi*, would take me back to a day of unresolved pain.

It was 14 October 2011 and my mother was dying in Basingstoke and North Hampshire Hospital. Pain revolves around the fact that there was a triangle of pretence surrounding her deathbed. My eldest child was not yet a year old and I was clinging to the fantasy that my mother would be around to dote on him. So my mind was focused on looking for flashes of hope and I was refusing to accept the reality of the vasculitis that was shutting her lungs down. My mother, a nurse herself, knew she was dying but, during that last conversation with her in the intensive care unit, I think she knew I couldn't go there. And neither could my sister, who tells me that the last conversation they had at the bedside was about birds – *birds*! I'm sure Mum would have empathized with these words from Tolstoy: 'What tormented Ivan Ilyich most was the deception, the lie, which for some reason they all accepted, that he was not dying but was simply ill. And he only need keep quiet and undergo a treatment and then something very good would result.'[1] So as my mother was about to be put under, with her lungs in shreds, we didn't have an honest conversation. Indeed, it was only when she was unconscious in intensive care that I said to her those things that I have rehearsed in my mind almost daily since her death: 'I love you; thank you; you've been wonderful; you've been so kind; goodbye; I'll see you again.' I'm sure a psychiatrist would tell me that this is a classic case of failure to get closure.

And then there were the medical staff. O Reader, I can't praise them highly enough. Mum was in that hospital for 100 days and they fought for her life night and day. But in that final week, my mother's dying felt like a medical event that was being defined and managed by medics, not a family's losing its cornerstone, during which some big things had to be said. Looking back, I'm convinced we needed to confront the truth of the situation. The triangle of pretence had to be torpedoed by a question such as 'What is your understanding of your condition?'

But it's not surprising that we didn't have that hard conversation, is it? In our culture, death has become such a taboo subject. Indeed, it was the sudden death of my godfather on 6 August 1982 in a cliff fall that made me realize that I'd never been spoken to about death, either at home or at school. No-one seemed to have any questions about it, until a maths teacher said to me, 'Look, Rico, if Christ got through death himself, he can get you through.' And yet, there I was, thirty years later and death was still a taboo subject.

I think we do three things with death in the West today. First, we *disengage* from it. So, just as my family did while I was growing up, we pretend it's not there. To give an example, my children have a super playground near our house and we love it. Yet, for centuries, it was the local cemetery. But no longer: the cemetery is a long way away behind a high wall up in Harrow. Second, we *distort* death, so we don't tell its full story. And this can be true in the church as well as in the world. At funerals, many of us have heard Canon Henry Scott Holland's poem 'Death is nothing at all'. The day after Mum died, we found out that Lucy was pregnant with our second son, Daniel; it didn't feel like death was nothing at all. So we disengage from death, we distort it and, lastly, we *despair* about it.

The people who famously confronted death, the ones who philosophically and emphatically contemplated the world with death and without God, were the French existentialists. They concluded that death made life meaningless. Jean-Paul Sartre wrote in his book *Nausea*: 'Nothing happens while you live. The scenery changes, people come in and go out, that's all. There are no beginnings. Days are tacked on to days without rhyme or reason, an interminable monotonous addition.'[2] So we don't know what to do with death and we, therefore, *disengage* from it, we *distort* it and we *despair* of it. And in the midst of this culture and that triangle of pretence, and after practising medicine for four decades, Professor John Wyatt has written this book. O how I wish I had read it before 14 October 2011. What a difference it would have made to me, my mother and, indeed, to the medics who treated her!

Do you know, as I read chapter 2, I actually got excited about preparing for my own death? I was excited about the spiritual challenge of dying well as a Christian, longing to follow in the footsteps of those who had thought about the art of dying. Never before had I prayed that I would die well. I do now regularly. And my mother – how I wish I could have led and helped effectively through death the person I loved so much and owed so much to! The regret is so profound that I have to stop myself thinking about it. But once more, I'm giving great thanks to God that John has headed towards the pain, and not away from it.

The Revd Rico Tice
Senior Minister for Evangelism
All Souls, Langham Place, London
and co-author of *Christianity Explored*

Acknowledgments

I would like to acknowledge my gratitude to the many people who have supported and contributed to the writing of this book. To my wife, Celia, who has patiently encouraged, supported and cajoled me over many months of slow progress. To my children and their spouses – JJ and Emma, Tim and Jess, Andrew and Beka – for their love, encouragement and criticism. To Alan and Sheila Toogood and their daughters Karen and Alison, who gave me permission to share their experiences and insights. To Rico Tice, for his encouragement, advice and wisdom. To the many friends and colleagues who read versions of the manuscript and provided invaluable comments, suggestions and corrections, including Ruth van den Broek, Jenny Brown, Ross and Elisabeth Bryson, Tess Butler, Elisabeth Chase, Terry Cox, Bishop Timothy Dudley-Smith, David and Jenny Gallagher, Alice Gerth, Janet Goodall, Ruth Guy, Michael Haughton, Dawn Hobson, Ella Kim, Jonathan Lewis, Kathy Myers, Karin and Vinoth Ramachandra, Malcolm and Anne Richard, Steve Richardson, Peter Saunders, Dimity Simmons, Philippa Taylor, Rick Thomas, David Turner, David Vardy and Rob Wilson.

A special thanks to the members of an informal advisory group: Robert Wilcox, Jenny Brown, James Tomlinson, and Steve and Dot Beck.

Finally, I am indebted to Eleanor Trotter of Inter-Varsity Press, for her patience and encouragement over many delays and for her invaluable advice and editorial guidance, and to Suzanne Mitchell for her excellent copy-editing. Of course, I retain responsibility for any errors and inaccuracies that remain.

Introduction

The news came as an unexpected and terrible shock. My father, who had been living alone since the death of my mother, had been discovered dead at home. I can still remember the sense of bewilderment and unreality. Years later it still hurts that I was unable to have a last conversation with my father, to tell him how much I loved him and how thankful I was for all that he had given me. None of us can know in advance when we might suddenly lose a loved one, nor how our own lives will end, but that means we need to think about it now, when we have the opportunity.

I have written this book as a doctor who has cared for many people both at the beginning and at the end of life, and who has wrestled for many years with the complex ethical and medical issues around life and death. I am also a son who has lost both parents, and a Christian believer who wants to know more about what it means to die well, and to die faithfully and honestly, in the light of the Christian good news. You too may share this faith, or you may be someone looking on from the outside. Either way, I hope you will find this book helpful and relevant.

Of course, it is never easy to think and talk about death, particularly about our own mortality, so congratulations on getting this far and at least starting the introduction to this book! I hope you will continue with me on this journey. The truth is that most people are unprepared for dying and do not want to think about it. Yet I have come to believe that this is a desperately important issue for all of us.

If you ask how they would like to die, most people today will say: 'I want to die in my bed while I am asleep. I don't want any warning, any premonition, any awareness. I just want to go out suddenly, like a light.' Yet the strange thing is that, if you were to go back four hundred years and ask people the same question, they would generally agree that sudden, unexpected death was the *worst possible* way to die. To be catapulted into eternity with no chance to prepare yourself, no chance to say goodbye, no chance to ask for forgiveness or to ensure your loved ones were provided for, no chance to prepare yourself to meet your Maker – what a terrible way to die.

So why have attitudes to dying changed so radically, and what can we learn from the way in which Christians of previous generations faced their own deaths? This book is intended to provide answers to these questions.

I have written the book for people who want to start to think about how their lives on earth are going to end and what it might involve. Perhaps you have received a diagnosis of what doctors call a 'life-limiting illness'. Or perhaps you simply recognize that you are getting older and you want to make sure that you are prepared for whatever might come next.

Perhaps you are a relative, a friend or a carer of someone who is coming to the end of life, and you are concerned about how to support him or her and what the future might hold. If so, this book is also for you. Appendix 1 is specifically intended for relatives and carers.

Whatever your situation, I can understand that you may feel anxious thinking about these issues. But, over the years, as I have had the privilege of talking about death and dying with many people, I have found that the most powerful and pervasive fears of all are fears of the unknown and the undiscussed. When we face these issues honestly and openly together, we can see that many of our darkest fears are out of touch with reality. The terrible fears of the night are so much easier to face in the bright light of day. The apostle John teaches us that we should 'walk in the light' (1 John 1:7), and one way we do this is by sharing our deepest fears and anxieties with those who love us and whom we can trust. My prayer is that this book will help you to do that.

Maybe you have watched a loved one, perhaps a parent or spouse, struggle with terminal illness or dementia, and you have wondered whether death would not be preferable to prolonged survival. My aim is to look honestly at the challenges and trials that may come at the end of life. But I also want to point out the strange and wonderful opportunities that dying well can bring. Internal growth, the healing of relationships, gratitude, laughter, finding forgiveness, fulfilling dreams: dying is not all loss, and it need not all be doom and gloom.

The first chapter looks at the topic of dying in the modern world, including the modern trend of the 'medicalization' of death, and the impact of medicine and hospital care on the experience of dying. We also look at changing attitudes towards suicide and the recent phenomenon of 'death cafés'.

The second, extremely brief, chapter introduces the *ars moriendi*, the 'art of dying', a Christian tradition from the late medieval period that provides a framework for the remainder of the book.

Chapter 3 looks at the surprising opportunities for internal growth and healing that are offered by dying well, while the following chapter looks at the most important fears and temptations that dying can give rise to, and what we can do to prepare for these.

Chapter 5 looks at some practical issues, particularly the importance of clear communication with health professionals and relatives. Chapter 6 looks at how we can learn from the example of Jesus himself about dying well, and focuses in particular on the words he spoke on the cross. Chapter 7 looks beyond the dying process to the scriptural hope of the resurrection and of the coming new heaven and earth.

The final section of the book provides material for carers, relatives and friends, together with additional resources, including prayers and suggestions for further reading.

As I have written these words and reflected on how I might experience death in the future, I have been conscious that my own faithfulness lags a long way behind the theory and I am at risk of hypocrisy and pretence. But I want to learn more of what it means to live well now in order that I may die well in the future, and this is also my prayer for you as a reader of this book.

So what does it mean to die well in a world of medical technology and patient choice? Why do so many people end their lives in hospital surrounded by impersonal machinery and anonymous professionals? What are the challenges and the opportunities that will meet us as we come to the end of our lives, and what can we learn from the countless Christian believers who have gone before us?

Dying in the modern world

In 2013 Nelson Mandela, the South African statesman who had given so much of his life to the cause of peace, lay in a critical care unit. He was ninety-four years old and had suffered from a range of chronic and distressing medical conditions for years. I was struck by the newspaper headlines around the world: 'Fears Grow for Nelson Mandela'; 'Family Gathers as Fears Grow for "Critical" Mandela'. One newspaper article reported, 'Nelson Mandela spent a second night in [a] critical condition in hospital on Monday night, with his family members, compatriots and well-wishers worldwide fearing that the anti-apartheid icon is about to lose his final struggle.'[1]

I found myself reflecting on the strangeness of this reaction, and wondering what exactly were the 'growing fears' about? There was no doubt that there were countless millions around the world who wished Mandela well, but what were they so fearful about? Was it so fearful a prospect that a frail ninety-four-year-old with multiple chronic illnesses might actually die? Was it really terrifying that the 'final struggle' of modern technological medicine against disease and death would be lost? Why should an extremely elderly man's dying be framed in the violent terms of 'struggle' and 'battle'?

Dying then and now

To many people today, disease and death are the enemy, and we are now part of a battle, fighting against the ancient enemy with all the powerful tools of modern technology. Death and dying used to take place in the home. At the beginning of the twentieth century, fewer than 15% of all deaths occurred in an institution, such as a hospital or nursing home. The overwhelming majority of people died in their own homes, with family, children and friends present at the bedside. Certainly, an elderly and much-revered leader like Nelson Mandela would have died at home, surrounded by his family, servants and well-wishers.[2]

Now, though, the focus has shifted to the hospital, and death has become medicalized. When we become seriously ill, we expect to be admitted to hospital. We expect treatment with the latest technology, wonder drugs and brilliant surgery. We know that modern medicine can provide wonderful, even miraculous, cures, and we expect to have access to the very best and most up-to-date treatments. After all, we do not go to hospital in order to die; we go there to get better.

The reality, of course, is that the battle against death is doomed to ultimate failure. Sometimes doctors, patients and relatives enter into a joint deception to avoid discussing the likelihood of death. The doctors do not want to discuss the possibility of 'failure'; the relatives do not want to destroy the patient's hope; and the patient is clinging on to the possibility of a medical miracle. Instead of open and honest discussion about the likelihood that death is approaching, there is a strange and ultimately damaging game of pretence.

Of course, I do not want to romanticize the experience of dying in the Victorian era. Medical techniques for pain relief and symptom control were rudimentary, and many people must have faced a prolonged and distressing end. I, for one, am intensely grateful for the extraordinary advances that have occurred in the medical care of the dying over the last century. (We will look briefly at those medical advances later.) But it is clear that, just one hundred years ago, dying at home was entirely normal and commonplace. Now, in the UK, only one in five will die at home. Just over half will end their lives in a hospital, about one in six will die in a care home and only one in twenty will die in a hospice.[3]

The problem is that it is the medical team who tell us what treatments are available for our condition, and the natural assumption is that we will be compliant patients in the unceasing battle against death, passive recipients of whatever therapies are available. The battle continues until the medical professionals decide that further treatment is hopeless. And then we die. Death has become defined by what doctors can and cannot do.

Dying has become a medical event.

As theologian Allen Verhey put it, 'The body of the dying person has become the battlefield where heroic doctors and nurses wage their war against death.'[4] I find this a striking and uncomfortable sentence, illustrating the passivity and depersonalization that modern medicine can foster. The unique person, with all the wonder and mystery of life history, loved ones, joys and sorrows, has become invisible. Instead there is just a body and an unceasing battle between medical technology and death. But dying in the midst of a battlefield is not a pleasant way to die.

There seems to be an epidemic of medical overtreatment spreading across the world. Sometimes it seems to be driven by medical arrogance and machismo. Sometimes there are perverse incentives for doctors or for hospitals that reward expensive but futile and burdensome treatments. Sometimes medical overtreatment is driven by doctors' inexperience or by fear of litigation. But even very experienced doctors may persist with overtreatment because of a sense that death represents a failure of medical skill and professionalism. If we buy into the modern medical narrative of an unceasing struggle against disease and death, it seems we are condemning ourselves to die as passive hostages in a battle waged by impersonal professionals.

After Mandela's death Bishop Desmond Tutu, Mandela's lifelong friend and confidant, spoke out: 'The manner of Nelson Mandela's prolonged death was an affront. I have spent my life working for dignity for the living. Now I wish to apply my mind to the issue of dignity for the dying.'[5] Ironically, Desmond Tutu then went on to argue that the only way to avoid the passivity and powerlessness of dying in a medicalized system was to legalize assisted suicide. This way all people would have the option to take control of their own destiny by killing themselves.

From the perspective of Desmond Tutu, we are confronted with a tragic and uncomfortable choice: either we die as passive hostages in an impersonal medical battlefield, or we seize control in the only way open to us, by committing suicide. But this is a strange, and frankly distorted, way of viewing the options at the end of life. Is there not a better way?

If there is to be better care of the dying, doctors and health professionals must recognize the limitations of their technology and their abilities: that there are limits to what doctors can and should do in the quest for healing and the preservation of life. And we have to recognize that those limits are not there because of failures in medical technology or professional skill. No; those limits come from the nature of our humanity – from the fact that we are fragile, dependent beings who are subject to disease, ageing and physical decline.

In fact, it could be argued that one of the primary roles of medical professionals in our society is to teach modern people about the limits that come from our physical nature. This is what theologian Stanley Hauerwas has called 'the wisdom of the body'. Disease provides an opportunity for learning more about the given-ness and limitations of our physical nature:

> Medicine can be viewed as an educational process for both doctor and patient, in which each is both teacher and learner. It is from patients that physicians learn the wisdom of the body. Both physicians and patients must learn that each of them is subject to a prior authority – the authority of the body. . . . [M]edicine represents a way of learning to live with finitude.[6]

The effect of religious beliefs on end-of-life treatment

From the perspective of the Christian faith, I will argue that the medicalization of death should be resisted. Dying should not be a medical event. Dying is an event that encompasses every aspect of life, and because (whether we like it or not) we are spiritual beings, death is a spiritual event. Yet one of the strange paradoxes of modern healthcare is that some Christian believers, as they approach the end of their lives, seem to cling on to powerful medical technology, even when it can bring no benefit.

Several research groups based in the USA have investigated the impact of patients' religious beliefs on the medical treatment they received as death approached.[7] Surprisingly, the researchers found that 'religious coping behaviour' was associated with a markedly *increased* preference for receiving all possible medical treatment, even when it had no chance of prolonging life. Religious patients were more likely to die in an intensive care unit, receiving full life support to the very end, than those who stated that they did not have religious beliefs.

Why was this? Some religious people said they believed that only God could decide when a patient should die, hence to refuse any possible treatment was 'tantamount to euthanasia'. Others said they believed they had to carry on with maximal treatment to the very end, in case God was going to do a miracle. Some said that accepting palliative care meant 'giving up on God'.

But can we really believe that dying in an intensive care unit, surrounded by the impersonal technology of infusion devices, monitors and life-support machinery, is the best way for a Christian believer to end his or her life on earth?

Suicide and self-determination

Like Desmond Tutu referred to above, some have argued that the answer to medicalization is to seize control. The author Terry Pratchett said, 'I believe passionately that any individual should have the right to choose, as far as it is possible, the time and the conditions of their death. I think it's time we learned to be as good at dying as we are at living.'[8] Pratchett was a high-profile campaigner for the legalization of assisted suicide, the legal right of all human beings to take their own lives with professional medical assistance.

Philosopher John Harris argues that autonomy, the ability and freedom to make choices about how we die – in his words, 'shaping our own lives for ourselves' – is what gives value to our existence.[9] Others have argued that each individual life story should be like a beautiful novel. I tell my own story, choosing each line and each chapter as I go along. If I cannot control my own death, that might mar the whole story of my life, just as a bad ending can ruin a beautiful novel. So I must be free to end my life in my own way, in a way that fits my life story.

The current arguments about assisted suicide are complex, as discussed in more length in *Right to Die?*, my companion volume. Behind the idea of individual autonomy is a deep individualism that stems historically from the European Enlightenment. Each person is regarded as something like a nation state with a single sovereign. This can lead to a bleak and lonely perspective. Ultimately, I am alone, locked inside my own body, making my own choices. And suicide can start to seem possible, and even attractive, from this perspective of cosmic loneliness.

It is very striking that, although suicide has been celebrated and honoured in many non-Christian cultures, it has nearly always been opposed by Christian believers. It is never glorified in the Bible, but instead seen as an act of hopelessness and despair, for example, in the tragic ends of King Saul, the first king of Israel, and Judas Iscariot. Despite this, as I have written elsewhere, it is clear that suicidal thoughts are not uncommon among God's people. Elijah wanted to die, but was sent on a sabbatical instead. Jeremiah wished he had died in his mother's womb, but discovered that God had plans for good and not for evil, to give 'a future and a hope' (Jeremiah 29:11). Job also wished he had never been born, but learnt that God was infinitely greater than his own perceptions.

As we will see in chapter 4, while suicidal thoughts may represent a temptation for some Christian believers as they come to the end of their lives, it is my profound conviction that we should resist this temptation, because it stems from despair, not from faith and hope.

The natural death movement

Elisabeth Kübler-Ross was a Swiss-born psychiatrist whose 1969 book *On Death and Dying* pioneered what came to be known as the 'natural death' or 'death awareness' movement.[10] Her book outlined five stages of grief – denial, anger, bargaining, depression and acceptance – that she argued many people experienced when faced with the reality of their impending deaths. It has to be said that there is little empirical evidence in support of the five stages described by Kübler-Ross, and most experienced doctors and counsellors do not employ this framework in a rigorous way.

In conscious opposition to the medicalization of dying, the natural death movement insisted that, since death could not be avoided, it must not be denied. Death was part of nature; it was 'natural'. Several different meanings can be detected in this slogan. One emphasized the biological cycles of nature. All living animals have a cycle of birth, life and death – spring, summer, autumn and winter. We come into the world, we develop and grow, we flourish, we age, we deteriorate and ultimately we die. This is the cycle of nature, and so death is natural, the ecology of the natural order. We have to die so that others can be born.

But the movement emphasized that there was more to death than the biological reality. In 1975 Kübler-Ross edited a book entitled *Death: The Final Stage of Growth* in which she wrote: 'Growing is the human way of living, and death is the final stage in the development of human beings. . . . We must allow death to provide a context for our lives, for in it lies the meaning of life and the key to our growth.'[11] Here

Kübler-Ross is claiming that dying is part of the process of self-realization; it provides the meaning of life and the essential key by which we can realize our inherent potential. This exalted view of the value of dying seems remarkably high-flown and very far from the unglamorous experiences of many at the end of life.

Theologian Allen Verhey argued that the death awareness movement, as started in the 1960s, was a modern retrieval of the nineteenth-century Romantic movement.[12] Romanticism was a reaction to the Enlightenment's emphasis on reason and science as a way to master nature, and in the same way the death awareness movement reacted against the medicalization and depersonalization of dying.

But, as Verhey and others have argued, the problem with the movement's mantra that 'death is natural' is its denial of the *wrongness* of death. The cycle of nature can bring comfort and consolation, but it is only so much help when I consider my own impending death, or the impending death of an infinitely precious, cherished and irreplaceable loved one. Death remains an autobiographical event, an event in someone's story, but it is a destructive event. Winter moves on to spring – but the person is gone, and the aching arms are empty. It is not enough to say that 'death is natural'. We need a more profound response that acknowledges the terrible reality, that sees the evil that death represents and looks towards the Christian hope that death will one day be destroyed.

Death cafés

A relatively recent initiative to encourage openness about death and the process of dying involves informal meetings dedicated to 'cake, tea and the discussion of death'. In 2004

the Swiss sociologist Bernard Crettaz organized the first
death café in Neuchâtel, Switzerland, with the aim of
breaking the 'tyrannical secrecy' surrounding the topic
of death.

The death café is not a physical location, but an event
involving a handful of people hosted at someone's house. The
concept has spread around the world; by 2017 there were over
4,400 death café events in forty-eight countries. The official
website describes the process in simple terms: 'At a Death
Cafe people, often strangers, gather to eat cake, drink tea and
discuss death. Our objective is "to increase awareness of death
with a view to helping people make the most of their (finite)
lives".'[13]

Unlike the death awareness movement, death cafés claim
to have no underlying agenda, objectives or themes. The
popularity and level of interest in the events reflect a deep
hunger to talk honestly about the topic. As Jon Underwood,
a British council worker who coordinated the movement,
put it,

> In my experience, when people talk about death and dying,
> all their pretences disappear. You see people's authenticity
> and honesty among strangers. Although it might sound
> really weird to say you attend a death cafe, it just feels very
> normal.[14]

As I have given talks and led discussions on the topic of death
and dying, I too have sensed a deep hunger for authenticity
and honest discussion. It seems sad that the Christian church
or local Christian community is not generally seen as an
appropriate place in which these discussions can take place.
How can we help strangers to talk about dying if we cannot
even talk about it among ourselves?

Christian thinking about death

There is a strange ambivalence about Christian attitudes to death. On the one hand, it is absolutely clear in the biblical narrative that death is an enemy: indeed, death is the ultimate enemy that continually threatens and besieges humankind. In biblical thought, human death is not an original part of God's creation order; in that sense, it is not 'natural'. Death is a mysterious and terrible interruption into the nature of being. The deep intuition that we share – that physical death (especially the death of a child or young person) is an outrage, an alien interruption into the goodness of reality – reflects the original creation order. Similarly, the inexpressible longing we have for eternity, for stability, for freedom from decay, reflects our created nature. We were not intended to die; we were made to live for ever. That is why Paul teaches that the risen Christ will ultimately destroy death, the 'last enemy' (1 Corinthians 15:26).

In its ceaseless struggle against death, modern medicine is bearing witness in advance to the ultimate destruction of death. The medical struggle is witnessing to the goodness of the creation and the goodness of bodily life with all its glories and its vulnerabilities. In my own medical career I remember days and nights spent in the intensive care unit, battling to hold death at bay from a single tiny precious life in an incubator. Yes, it was worth it. Death is an enemy to fight against with all our strength, perseverance and courage.

And yet . . . In the biblical narrative the human lifespan is limited, not just as a curse, but out of God's grace. Adam and Eve, in their fallen and degraded state, were driven out of the Garden of Eden to prevent them from eating the fruit of the tree of life and living for ever. And to prevent their return and capture of the fruit by force of arms, cherubim and a flaming sword were set 'to guard the way to the tree of life' (Genesis 3:24). The biblical narrative makes plain that to live for ever in a fallen state is not a blessing, but a curse.

So, in God's mysterious providence, death may on occasion change from being an enemy. It may become a release from an existence trapped in a fallen and decaying body – in C. S. Lewis's wonderful words, 'a severe mercy'.[15] Christian attitudes to death must always reflect this strange ambivalence. Even though human death is fundamentally an evil to be fought against, a reality that must never be sought intentionally, it may also at times be accepted as a sign of God's mercy.

Like many other Christian believers, I hesitate to talk about a 'good death', but I do believe that we can learn to die well, and that is obviously what this book is all about.

The art of dying

Let us go back a bit. Europe in the fourteenth and fifteenth centuries was a frightening place. In 1348–1349 the Black Death swept across the continent, killing more than a quarter of the entire population, and remained a threatening presence throughout the following centuries. The dreadful disease could enter a village or town without warning, and no-one, rich or poor, was safe from its ravages. It is not surprising that many people in this period seemed to be morbidly obsessed with death and with the way that plague could ambush the living at a moment's notice and drag them to their deaths.

It was in this climate that documents entitled *Ars moriendi*, which simply means 'The Art of Dying', started to circulate.[1] Historians have estimated that at least 300 different manuscripts were produced during the Middle Ages. This form of writing started in pre-Reformation Europe, but similar documents and books for the dying continued to be produced through to the seventeenth and eighteenth centuries, including some by Anglican, Lutheran and Calvinist writers.

The *Ars moriendi* were self-help manuals for those who were dying. In times of plague you could not be confident that a priest would be present to hear your confession and help you to prepare for the end. So the *Ars moriendi* could be read while you were still healthy, but also kept for use during the final days and hours.

Over the years, a standard format emerged. It usually started with a section entitled 'A Commendation of Death' – a bizarre-sounding concept to modern ears. Then there was a section with warnings to the dying person of the temptations he or she might confront and how they should be resisted. The temptations were often illustrated by vivid woodcut images showing the dying believer lying on a bed with demons floating around, whispering temptations, or seeking to seize the person and drag him or her bodily to hell.

This section was followed by a short catechism on repentance, with questions and answers giving the assurance of God's pardon. The subsequent section used the dying Christ as a model for one's own dying and suggested prayers for use by the dying person. The final section emphasized the importance of these preparations for death and also provided prayers for those caring for the dying person.

The *Ars moriendi* were strikingly different from many of the religious documents circulating at the time because they emphasized the importance of self-help for lay people. Allen Verhey suggested that a modern equivalent title would be *Dying for Dummies*! Instead of passively accepting the ministrations of priests and carers, the dying person was exhorted to action, engagement and preparation for faithful dying.

Of course, our world is vastly different from the one in which the *Ars moriendi* circulated. But perhaps we too are at risk of facing the dying process with passivity and despair. It is not the absence of priests and clergy that is the problem. It is more the dominance of the medical professionals and the hospital systems that pressurize dying people into docility and hopelessness. Dying has become a medical event which is defined and managed by the medical professionals. As we saw in the previous chapter, our bodies can become the battleground on which impersonal medical technology wages war against death. We, the patients, are in danger of being turned into passive and helpless recipients. We need help to understand how we can again become active participants in the process of dying.

It is hundreds of years since the Black Death struck Europe. Scholarly works on the *Ars moriendi* are starting to appear and the question of what it means for Christian people to die faithfully is being discussed with renewed energy. What would happen if we tried to translate the medieval art of dying into our world, a world of technological medicine and care pathways for dying people? Or is our world so different that there is nothing we can learn from this quaint lost tradition?

We need to learn to become active participants in the process of dying.

This has been just a brief look at the documents and their format, setting the scene and offering context. Join me now on a journey of exploration into the opportunities, challenges and tests that dying can bring, to see what, if anything, we can learn from the past.

The opportunities that dying well may bring

Can death really be a friend? We noted in the previous chapter that the *Ars moriendi* documents often started with a bizarre-sounding section entitled 'A Commendation of Death'. The wretchedness of life on this earth was contrasted with the blessings of the life to come. Death was leaving the prison, ending the exile, throwing off the heavy burden of the body, escaping perils. As a result, death was to be welcomed and received as a 'well-beloved and trusted friend'.

Modern scholars suggest that the medieval tradition was heavily influenced by the thinking of the ancient Stoics, which was enjoying renewed prominence through the Renaissance movement in southern Europe.[1] The Stoics saw every event of life as governed by divine reason; therefore, anything that occurred, including suffering, dying and death, should be accepted with equanimity and cheerfulness. It is interesting to note the many parallels between the ancient Stoic thinking and the modern natural death movement of Elisabeth Kübler-Ross and others. Like the Stoics, the natural death movement advocates the virtues of acceptance and an element of resignation in the face of suffering and death.

But, as we have already seen, both the Old and the New Testaments have a very different perspective on the nature of death. In the poetic imagery of the Genesis creation narratives, Adam and Eve had access in the Garden of Eden not only to almost all the other fruit within the garden, but also to the tree of life. Within the biblical narrative it seems that Adam and Eve could have chosen to eat the fruit of that tree and live for ever. Instead, they chose to disobey God and eat the fruit of the one tree that was forbidden. The very fact that the tree of life was in the garden and its fruit was there to be eaten suggests that God's original intention for human beings was everlasting life. In biblical thought, the death of human beings, in all its horror and mystery, is not 'natural'; it is not the way it was meant to be. Death is a mysterious and dreadful enemy, a threat, a destroyer. We were not intended to die; we were made to live for ever.

Death: an enemy

This is where authentic Christian thinking has to diverge from the approach of the natural death movement. Yes, death is part of our fallen human nature, a painful reality that we have to accept. But we cannot join in with the fatalistic acceptance of the cycle of life and death, agreeing that death is as good as life. Death remains an alien intrusion into reality. On this point, modern medicine gets it right and the natural death movement gets it wrong. It is not an accident that the historical roots of modern healthcare were embedded in a Christian understanding of what it means to be human. From the time of the early church, and the first hospitals, which were linked to ancient monasteries, Christian doctors and nurses treated the human body with special wonder and respect because this was the form in which God chose to become flesh. They celebrated the goodness of human life and used their healing arts to overcome disease and suffering wherever possible.[2]

In its refusal to accept death and its ceaseless struggle against disease, modern technological healthcare is continuing to celebrate the goodness of bodily life and, although most healthcare professionals may not recognize it, they are in fact bearing witness in advance to the ultimate destruction of death. The enterprise of modern healthcare is a public statement that death is not natural and it will not have the last word. But, as we saw previously, the noble struggle in favour of life and against death can so easily become distorted and lead to unanticipated and damaging consequences. Perhaps we need to recover some of the wisdom that the old *Ars moriendi* documents displayed in their 'Commendation of Death'.

The process of dying can . . . be redeemed and turned into a source of . . . blessing.

Yes, death is evil, but the process of dying can, by the grace of God, be redeemed and turned into a source of strange and unlooked-for blessing.

Dying well: opportunities and adventures

Christian physician John Dunlop, who has had long clinical experience of caring for dying people, wrote,

> One thing I have learned is that dying well is rarely a
> coincidence. Rather it results from choices made throughout

life. After all, dying well is nothing more than living well right up till the end.[3]

Author Rob Moll writes,

> *'Dying well is nothing more than living well right up to the end.'*

A good death requires more than practical caring. Relationships need completing and sometimes mending, faith needs nurturing, stories need telling. There is work to be done – the work of completing a life. There are goals to fulfil – such as writing a life story or working on some kind of life review to pass on to the next generations. There is saying goodbye and preparing myself spiritually.[4]

So, in line with the suggestions of these two authors, we shall look at a number of opportunities and adventures that dying well can bring. I have listed nine.

1. Internal spiritual growth

The Anglican Book of Common Prayer includes the following words:

> Sanctify, O Lord, the sickness of your servant *N*, that the sense of *his* weakness may add strength to *his* faith and seriousness to *his* repentance; and grant that *he* may live with you in everlasting life; through Jesus Christ our Lord. *Amen.*
> ('For the Sanctification of Illness')

The prayer assumes that a deep sense of weakness caused by illness can, by God's grace, lead both to strengthening of faith in Christ and to a more serious and genuine repentance.

It is a strange paradox of our human existence that internal growth is fostered by adversity. When our lives are smooth and untroubled, internal growth and development are less likely. But when we face new experiences, challenge and uncertainty, these are God-given opportunities for us to grow and make progress emotionally and spiritually.

This is a wonderful phenomenon that I have been privileged to witness on a number of occasions. From the outside, the body is deteriorating and the effects of disease or old age are becoming more and more obvious. But on the inside, the person's spirit seems to be growing; there is an internal clarity, even beauty.

Rico Tice, pastor-evangelist at All Souls Church, Langham Place, London, told me how, as a very inexperienced and junior pastor, he visited our mutual friend Stuart who was dying from advanced lymphoma. Stuart was a quiet and rather reserved person in his thirties, a professional musician who, until the cancer was diagnosed, had immersed himself in academic studies. But as he came to terms with his imminent death, he discovered new strength and spiritual vitality in the Christian hope. As Rico walked into Stuart's room, he blurted out the first thing that came into his head: 'So, Stuart, what's it like to be dying?'

Stuart gave him a look. 'Rico, Christ is risen. You may think the cross is precious to you, but think what it means to me. I'm going to be standing before him in three days' time.'

In the second letter to the Corinthians the apostle Paul uses the analogy of an earthen clay pot, the type that was often used to store and hide treasure in the ancient world:

> We have this treasure in jars of clay, to show that the surpassing power belongs to God and not to us. We are afflicted in every way, but not crushed; perplexed, but not driven to despair;

persecuted, but not forsaken; struck down, but not destroyed; always carrying in the body the death of Jesus, so that the life of Jesus may also be manifested in our bodies.

(2 Corinthians 4:7–10)

Our human bodies and personalities may appear to be just humble clay pots, but, by God's grace, deep within there is a priceless and inexhaustible treasure that cannot decay or be destroyed.

Paul goes on:

So we do not lose heart. Though our outer self is wasting away, our inner self is being renewed day by day. For this light momentary affliction is preparing for us an eternal weight of glory beyond all comparison, as we look not to the things that are seen but to the things that are unseen. For the things that are seen are transient, but the things that are unseen are eternal.

(2 Corinthians 4:16–18)

Rob Moll writes,

Spiritually a dying person is very much alive. . . . [The person is] outwardly wasting away but internally growing. . . . Spiritual growth at the end of life may involve a new awareness – a new understanding of the spiritual life or a reinvigorated devotional life. . . . Even Alzheimer's cannot touch the life of the spirit.

One of the profound spiritual lessons that dying has to teach us is to learn to see beyond the superficial appearance of our humanity to recognize the spiritual reality and beauty that lie beneath. In our materialistic and image-conscious culture, it is all too easy to focus on the 'things that are seen': the external, the superficial, the outer self. It is the outward appearance that tends to dominate our thoughts and preoccupations. When we see our own bodies, or those of the people we love most, deteriorating because of disease or ageing, becoming wrinkly, flabby and distorted, we are secretly appalled. But we need spiritual eyes to see that there is more here than meets the eye: by God's grace there is a hidden glory. Dying gives us an opportunity to devote new attention and concentration to the inner self that, by God's grace, can be renewed, restored and glorified for eternity.

Reflecting on the suffering of the biblical character Job, Don Carson writes,

> The reason for suffering is not rooted in the past, but in the future – it may not be punishment for past sins, but is designed to develop our characters. . . . God is less interested in answering our questions than in other things: securing our allegiance, establishing our faith, nurturing a desire for holiness.[5]

Rico Tice once visited Ann in hospital. Ann was an elderly single woman who had been a member of All Souls for many years, but now she was close to death. As Rico entered the ward, he gave her name to the nurse and asked where she was. The nurse replied, 'Oh, you mean Gabby – we all call her "the Angel Gabriel" because she shines!'

So dying well is an opportunity for focusing on the unseen realities more than the seen. But, through speaking to people as I prepared this book, I have realized that this is an opportunity for carers too. The Filipina author Evelyn Miranda-Feliciano writes,

> A dear friend . . . was diagnosed with cancer of the liver. Her family was too poor to enable her to stay in the hospital for prolonged treatment. So, she decided to wait for death at home.

'We better spend the money for the children's education,' she said unselfishly. I visited to pray with her regularly and was amazed to witness how her spirit glowed through a pain-wracked body. 'I am thankful to God for every bit of life I see around, even the wagging of the cow's tail that I see from my window,' I remember her say. I had wanted to be a comfort to her during my visits; instead I would go away comforted, my faith deepened by her.[6]

When someone dies well, there is an opportunity for spiritual growth for loved ones, relatives and friends. Many people have told me that their own faith in Christ was strengthened, deepened and made more concrete as they accompanied a dying believer during the last weeks, days and hours of his or her life.

2. Being thankful

Gratitude may seem to be a paradoxical response when facing a terminal illness. Surely bitterness and resentment would be more understandable?

Katie Bryson was a young and talented artist who had struggled with cancer from childhood. When she was in her late twenties she was diagnosed with an inoperable brain tumour. Her story is told in a short and moving book, *Dying Without Fear*, based on her journal and poems. In the book, Katie talks about her fears and concerns. But the book is suffused with gratitude for her family and for the experiences of her final weeks:

> Tonight we are in St Ives! A beautiful bed in a cosy cottage welcomes me this evening. . . . Thank you, Lord, that even when I'm tired and need to rest, the family can still have time together. Thank you, Lord, for this beautiful place and wonderful holiday time with all of us here!

Today I had times in my wheelchair, sitting at the harbour front painting, which I really enjoyed. . . . Thank you for today and your gift of life today.

Back to life in Birmingham, but life wherever it happens is a gift and blessing from God. Life for me might not be as long as it could be, but that does not mean that I am not grateful for every minute of it . . .

Katie's last journal entry, days before her death, said,

Good morning, Lord! Thanks for another day here full of You, Your life, Your hope, Your ways. It would be great if Toby could come out of hospital today. [And he did – having had his appendix removed.]

Lord, you know me inside out, you know my desires in this winter season. Most of all you know when I'm coming home, how I'm ready to come home any time. Please could you help me not to feel flat and hopeless sometimes and to remember that you are the God of hope, and the One on whom I can depend?[7]

Here are the words of Ruth van den Broek, a young Christian believer who has written movingly about her experience of living with cystic fibrosis:[8]

When it comes to dying well, gratitude has been one of the most transformative things for me. Gratitude for my body despite its brokenness, for my medical team despite their limits, for the decay of my lungs because it makes me notice and appreciate most of my waking breaths. A while back I started praying before I took medications, the way I do before food: 'Lord, Thank you for these medications. Thank you for the people who invented, prescribed and prepared them. Please bless the medications to my body and my body in your service.' I began to see them as the blessings they are. Gratitude has changed so much for me, even though I'm still not great at it.[9]

3. Healing, building, celebrating and completing relationships

Dying well is an opportunity for healing from the inside: it is an opportunity for broken relationships to be healed and restored, even after many years of fracture and hostility, and it is an opportunity for good relationships to be made stronger, more open and more honest. It is an opportunity for sharing from the heart, and for saying 'sorry' and 'thank you' to those who are closest to us.

To die well, I have to be at peace with God and . . . the most important people in my life.

In order to die well, I have to be at peace with God and at peace with the most important people in my life. Strangely and wonderfully, dying people are able to bless their loved ones by 'completing' or strengthening their most significant relationships. Ira Byock, an experienced hospice doctor, noted that

> patients who die most peacefully and families who felt enriched by the passing of a loved one tended to be particularly active in terms of their relationships and discussions of personal and spiritual matters. . . . It was as if dying from a progressive illness had provided them with opportunities to resolve and complete their relationships and get their affairs in order.[10]

Perhaps it is unhelpful to think that our relationships on earth can be 'completed'. Each of us is on a journey and we are being called onwards by God to the next stage of our pilgrimage. Perhaps our relationships will never be brought to their fullest potential this side of eternity. But it is surely right that we should try to avoid 'unfinished business'. Dying is a once-in-a-lifetime opportunity to mend, strengthen and celebrate our relationships and bonds with those whom we love.

4. *Finding forgiveness*

An older woman, whom I shall call Mary, was diagnosed with a very advanced and aggressive form of cancer. She had experienced a life of broken relationships, and her daughter described her as 'an intensely angry person' with a sharp and destructive tongue. Her daughter had found faith in Christ as a young adult, but Mary had always rejected and rebuffed any attempt to talk about God or the gospel.

But then came the sudden news that she had advanced cancer and only weeks to live. Sitting in the radiotherapy outpatients department, surrounded by other patients and relatives, she turned to her daughter and said, 'I've got three questions for you: How can I forgive? How can I be forgiven? And what is heaven like?'

For the first time, Mary talked about her hidden secret of having been abused as a child, and the shame, hurt, hatred and anger that had dominated her life. Mary's daughter gently shared about the person of Christ and his forgiveness, the fact that she could be 'wiped clean', and that heaven was a place of safety where nothing would be able to harm her again.

From that time in the outpatients department, Mary's life was changed. 'My mum was remade two weeks before she died,' said her daughter. 'I've never seen anything more radical in my life!'

Mary was admitted to a local nursing home for terminal care. In place of the earlier bitterness and resentment there was thankfulness. Her daughter remembers Mary's gratitude when she received a plate of puréed vegetables: 'I can't believe how kind you are to me,' Mary said. When sitting with her grandchildren, she wept. 'You've got no idea what it feels like to pray for the first time,' she said. 'I feel as though there's an external power to control my tongue. I have the power to choose what I want to say.'

Mary died barely two weeks after that conversation in the outpatients department, with her daughter holding her hand and singing hymns to her. As the end came, her daughter whispered to her, 'Your body isn't needed any more. You are going to receive a brand-new body.' And then, very gently, came the last breath.

Immediately after Mary's death, the nurses gathered in her room. 'This was an amazing lady! She was so grateful for everything, so kind, so gentle. She had no fear about dying. We've never seen anyone die like this!' And her daughter was able to share with them something of the grace and forgiveness that her mother had discovered in those precious last days of her life.

Dying well is an opportunity to find forgiveness, to be remade, to become a 'new creation', in the words of the apostle Paul. It is to hear the invitation in Stuart Townend's beautiful hymn:

Come lay your heavy load
Down at the Master's feet;
Your shame will be removed,
Your joy will be complete.
Come crucify your pride,
And enter as a child;
For those who bow down low
He'll lift up to His side.

What joy, what peace has come to us!
What hope, what help, what love![11]

5. Letting go

Dying well is an opportunity for me to let go of tasks that I will never complete and responsibilities that I can no longer maintain. It is a chance to accept that God is in control of my life and that I need to let go, particularly of those parts of my life where I am still desperately grasping on to the things of this earth.

But letting go is not as easy as it sounds. As we get older, there are many pleasures in and attachments to the material world and we may find it increasingly hard to let go.

John Dunlop writes,

> Many of the losses associated with ageing are inevitable and often forced upon us, but some things we can choose to give up voluntarily. When we can see the losses coming, I have observed that it is much better to recognize them, plan for them, and make changes somewhat gradually and proactively rather than waiting for a crisis to force a drastic change.[12]

We must learn to let go gradually and willingly.

It is very noticeable that many older people in Western societies find it extremely difficult to let go as they approach the end of life. Most people who are now in their eighties and nineties went through the Second World War and its aftermath. Many sacrificed everything just to get by and to provide for families and loved ones. They learnt not to rely on benefits or handouts; they worked, even struggled, to be self-sufficient. They developed an ethic of service for others, yet they abhorred the idea of depending on other people, 'of becoming a burden'. It is no wonder that they find it difficult to give things up. But dying well gives us an opportunity, by the grace of God, to learn to let go.

Perhaps the hardest part is saying goodbye to those whom we love most dearly. In his book *Life's Living toward Dying*, theologian Vigen Guroian writes,

> Death would not be so bitter were it not that love makes life so sweet. Nor would death inspire such fear and dread were it not that it cuts us off from those whom we love and who love us.[13]

It is hard for the dying to leave those they love, and equally hard for those who remain to let go of the dying. This is because love for those who are closest to us is one of the greatest gifts that God gives us in this world of constant change and challenge. So being torn apart from those whom we love is a kind of agony. This is true whether we feel torn from father or mother, brother or sister, son or daughter, or our closest friends. And for those who have been given the gift of marriage, there is a special pain in being separated from those with whom we have become 'one flesh'. Death involves a painful tearing apart of what was united. Here again is a stark reminder that death is an enemy.

John Dunlop reminds those approaching death to be sensitive and thoughtful about the impact that their illness may be having on their loved ones: 'I suggest to patients they simply say, "This illness of mine is forcing many changes in our family. How are you coping with it?"' This gives an opportunity for open and honest sharing that will help everyone bear the emotional demands of impending death.

But it is God's plan, as we learn to die well, for us to be progressively detached from earthly attachments, and (at least for a time) from earthly relationships, so that we can be prepared for the next phase of the journey. Yes, by God's grace, we will meet again in a completely new and different way in the new heaven and the new earth. This separation, however painful, is only temporary. But for now I am being called to focus on my Lord, my Redeemer and my Bridegroom. It is he who will close my eyes and it is he who will awaken me from sleep.

6. Leaving a legacy

Dying well is a time for thinking of those who come after us and an opportunity for focusing on their needs. This may include making financial and practical provision for our loved ones, but of course each of us can leave so much more than a financial legacy. We can pass on our heart concerns to them and provide a testimony to God's faithfulness.

This is a frequent theme in the Scriptures. David wrote,

> O God, from my youth you have taught me,
>   and I still proclaim your wondrous deeds.
> So even to old age and grey hairs,
>   O God do not forsake me,
> until I proclaim your might to another generation,
>   your power to all those to come.
> (Psalm 71:17–18)

> I will sing of the steadfast love of the LORD, for ever;
>   with my mouth I will make known your faithfulness
>   to all generations.
> (Psalm 89:1)

The writer of Deuteronomy put great emphasis on the importance of instructing the next generation:

> These words that I command you today shall be on your heart. You shall teach them diligently to your children, and shall talk

of them when you sit in your house, and when you walk by the
way, and when you lie down, and when you rise.
(Deuteronomy 6:6–7)

Dying provides an unparalleled opportunity to reflect on
the way that God has led and blessed us during our lives,
and the lessons we have learnt along the journey. It can be
extremely helpful to turn this reflection into a spiritual autobiography, either spoken or written, for the next generation.

My father spent considerable time in his last years writing
a detailed autobiography: how he had been converted to
Christianity, how he had met my mother and how God
had guided, protected and blessed him through a long life.
Sadly, he wasn't able to complete the task before he was
called home, suddenly and unexpectedly, as I have previously described. But, as I have reflected on it while writing
this book, I have understood more of the importance of
what he chose to do, and have gone back to read his words
again.

Some people choose to write letters to their loved ones to
be distributed after their deaths. I have read of dying people
writing letters to their children or grandchildren, to be given
to them at important life events like graduations or weddings.
And, of course, leaving a spiritual legacy is not only for
genetic children or grandchildren. We have responsibilities
towards our spiritual children, our closest friends and others
whom God has put in our way.

Shortly before they died, the Old Testament patriarchs had
an essential role in pronouncing a specially composed blessing
upon each of their children. There is no doubt that the individual blessings and prayers were never forgotten. Perhaps
this ancient tradition could be revived in a twenty-first-century
form. It might be helpful to reflect on and plan ahead of time

the words that would be most meaningful and encouraging for each individual.

7. Reordering priorities

Dying well is an opportunity for reordering priorities. It is a chance for me to show to others (and to myself) what is really important in my life. When Stuart, whom we met earlier, discovered that he had a terminal illness, he was absorbed in studying for a PhD. But he chose to abandon his studies so that he could use his final weeks in a very different manner. He told me that he wanted to write a letter to everyone he knew, explaining what was happening to him and sharing his faith and hope of eternal life with them in a personal way. When he first told me this, I was secretly astonished. This was not the Stuart I thought I knew. As I mentioned earlier, he was a quiet and rather introverted man who did not easily talk about himself or his deepest feelings. But dying had given him a new boldness and urgency.

Over those last weeks Stuart probably wrote more letters than he had done during the rest of his life. Diane, a close friend, said,

> He was constantly writing letters. He had a big list that he was working through. I think he wanted to share the confidence that he had in the face of death, with friends who didn't know Jesus and hadn't the same confidence – people he'd met over the years. He really was bursting to tell them about this hope that he had. He was always writing letters and he was always telling me who he had written to that day and who he needed to write to. And he hoped he wouldn't die before he'd got all those letters written.

Stuart also had an opportunity to speak to the student group at All Souls Church:

The time that he came down to speak to the students, you could have touched the atmosphere that night. Everybody was in tears, and they were, I think, just amazed at the bravery with which he was facing death. And just his strength and the assurance he had of where he was going – it really spoke to the students. We don't tend to think about our own death. But here was a young man who was absolutely struggling, the sweat was rolling off his face that night as he spoke, and he could hardly get a breath. Yet the glory and the joy with which he spoke just filled the room.

Richard Bewes, the rector of All Souls at the time, talked about Stuart:

The whole church knew what was happening. He had visited the student group; he had met with various groups in the church. And also, because he was one of our public musicians, a pianist, it meant that he was regularly on show. So it came to a head, finally. The last service I recall him taking part in was a massive communion service at which there were at least a thousand present. I was presiding and Stuart was playing the piano. And at some point, just before the breaking of the bread and the pouring out of the cup, I was able to say, 'It's wonderful we are all here from our different backgrounds. It's wonderful that here is Stuart playing the piano for us on this very important night.' And that meant there was a fellowship, a deep fellowship of prayer, and of suffering and of the cross. The cross was there at the centre, and we felt that we were all gathered together with Stuart at the cross. Everybody knew that he was dying, and I suppose most of us knew that this was perhaps the last time we would see him among us. But there was fellowship in that too and a deep understanding.[14]

At his memorial service many were present who had received a special letter from Stuart: a letter in which he poured out his heart to them, in an unusually open and forthright way. And, sitting in that memorial service, I suddenly realized that, in a strange sense, I was envious of Stuart. He had had an opportunity to write those letters that most of us will never write, to say those things to his friends that most of us will never say. Stuart died well. Those last three months were a wonderfully rich, profound experience for him and for his many friends.

8. Fulfilling dreams

You may be surprised to discover that dying well is an opportunity to fulfil dreams. Many people have found that it is only when they are dying that their lifelong dreams come to the fore. Those dreams can be acknowledged and sometimes fulfilled. So perhaps for you, dying well is not a time to focus on 'must', 'ought' and 'should'; it is a time to focus on 'I'd just love to . . .' and 'Wouldn't it be wonderful if . . . ?'

Of course, those dreams will be different for each one of us, and rightly so. For Katie Bryson, mentioned earlier, it was the dream of having a family holiday in Cornwall, finding opportunities to paint and use her creative gifts, and watching the sun set over the sea one last time. For my friend Karin Ramachandra, it was a special railway trip to Jaffna in Sri Lanka. For Stuart, it was writing heartfelt letters.

> 'You matter to the last moment of your life, and we will do all we can not only to help you die peacefully, but also to live until you die.'

Cicely Saunders, the Christian visionary behind modern palliative care, said, 'You matter because you are you. You matter to the last moment of your life, and we will do all we can not only to help you die peacefully, but also to live until you die.'[15] Those words 'to live until you die' became a slogan of the palliative care movement. Acknowledging, recognizing and expressing our dreams is part of how we live until we die.

9. Preparing to meet our Lord and Saviour

I had known Alan Toogood for many years. We had met at All Souls Church and we had both, in different ways, faced the implications of sudden illness and unexpected loss. It was out of the experience of shared grief that he became one of my closest and dearest friends. After some years he was diagnosed with cancer, which steadily progressed until it was clear that the disease was at a terminal stage.

When he was admitted to hospital it was a privilege to be able to visit him. We were able to share from the heart, to laugh and to weep together. Just a few weeks earlier I had heard a talk from my friend Philippa Taylor, an elite long-distance runner, explaining how to cope with the phenomenon of 'hitting the wall', the moment when exhaustion and fatigue hit towards the end of a race. These are her words:

> From my own experience of competitive racing, I often particularly struggle physically and mentally at about three quarters of the way in, in both long and short races. It's then that I want to slow down, even stop. It can be really tough. But I've learnt to do *two things*: firstly, to stay in the moment – in other words, don't think about the next few miles, how far there still is to go, or how I'm feeling, and instead to just concentrate on the current kilometre or mile, to 'stay in that moment'. And secondly, I think about crossing the finish line – I think of how I'll feel, of the time I want to achieve, of the cake (!) and of the

prize (hopefully!). I try to actually picture it all. It's still not easy, but both those strategies really help to keep me going.[16]

Alan also had been a marathon runner all his life. He 'hit the wall' in his final illness. He was feeling exhausted and was just hanging on. So I shared Philippa's words with him. 'That's right,' he said. 'That's exactly what you have to do when you are racing. And that's what I have to focus on now.'

It is helpful to reflect on these two ways of coping as we tire of the endurance race that we are running.

The sacrament of the present moment

First, we are called to focus on the present moment. What does that mean in reality? I think it means consciously choosing not to think about what might happen the next day, the next week or the next month, wondering how I will cope and whether I will give up entirely. It is choosing not to think about all the things I have left undone, the tasks I have failed to complete, the people I have failed to contact. Instead, I try to focus my entire attention on what is happening at this present moment. This may sound like a version of the modern idea of 'mindfulness'. But in Christian thinking, the practice is very different. I focus on what God himself is giving to me in this present moment.

Jean Pierre de Caussade was a French Catholic spiritual director of the eighteenth century. He wrote a book called *Abandonment to Divine Providence* which became a spiritual classic. His central insight was that whatever was happening in the present moment could be regarded as a special spiritual gift, a sacrament, a visible sign of God's invisible grace. This did not mean that whatever was happening was good in itself. The present moment might encompass all manner of difficult, challenging and evil realities.

But it is orthodox biblical Christian teaching that God's providence extends to every moment of our lives. God has, therefore, allowed this present moment to occur. The Gospels reveal that Jesus lived fully in each and every moment of his life: 'My food is to do the will of him who sent me and to accomplish his work' (John 4:34). It seems that he did not spend time worrying about what the future held – although, of course, he knew that there was a baptism that was coming and fire that was waiting to be kindled. Rather, he took each moment as a gift from his Father.

The apostle Paul emphasized that God's love is expressed in his providence in the minutiae of life: '. . . in all things God works for the good of those who love him, who have been called according to his purpose' (Romans 8:28 NIV). As many Bible teachers have emphasized, this does not mean that everything that happens is good. It may be a terrible evil. But out of his love and grace God is able to use even terrible evil for good: he can redeem it – bring blessing and healing out of pain, suffering and despair.

Jean Pierre de Caussade taught that, even if the present moment seems profoundly difficult and unwanted, we should learn to see it as a new opportunity to experience God's presence and his providential love for and care over us:

> There is not a moment in which God does not present Himself under the cover of some pain to be endured, of some consolation to be enjoyed, or of some duty to be performed. All that takes place within us, around us, or through us, contains and conceals His divine action.[17]

In other words, God hides himself behind the tiniest events of everyday life, and I need to find him by abandoning myself to his wish to give me this present moment, and to discover what he wants to give me in this moment.

I am aware that this may seem rather mystical and unrealistic. It goes against the grain of our activist and problem-solving instincts. If there is a problem, we fix it, or we get someone else to fix it. If there is a challenge, we learn how to overcome it. But it does seem to me that there is a deep spiritual truth in the concept of the sacrament of the present moment, particularly as we face the fatigue and weariness of the marathon journey that seems never to be coming to an end. We choose to take our thoughts away from how many miles lie ahead of us and from the ever-present temptation to despair, and we focus on the grace and reality of God who hides behind the present moment.

Focusing on the finishing line
Second, in the words quoted above, Philippa Taylor said that she deliberately thinks about the experience of crossing the finishing line. She imagines the experience in her mind. She tries to anticipate those feelings of achievement, joy, satisfaction and relief that will come as she crosses that line. She visualizes sinking her teeth into cake and drinking hot tea, and the experience of standing on the podium and receiving the prize.

Philippa also told me how much she loves the passage in Hebrews 12 that uses the same imagery:

> Therefore, since we are surrounded by so great a cloud of witnesses, let us . . . lay aside every weight, and sin which clings so closely, and let us run with endurance the race that is set before us, looking to Jesus, the founder and perfecter of our faith . . .
>
> (Hebrews 12:1–2)

Here is the same metaphor of the endurance race. But it is not a solitary race. Instead, we are surrounded by a great crowd of invisible onlookers cheering us on. They are the faithful believers who have run this race before us and who, by faith, were able to endure to the end. And instead of visualizing chocolate cake (!), we are called to think of the One who is waiting to receive us with inexpressible joy at the end of the race. Fifteen centuries ago, Boethius wrote those beautiful words: 'Thou art the journey . . . and the journey's end.'[18]

I had the privilege of spending another precious time with Alan Toogood just hours before he died in hospital. Neither he nor I knew how close he was to the finishing line. His friends David and Jenny Gallagher had given him a little hand-carved wooden cross, a 'hand-cross', designed to be held in the palm of the hand. This little cross came to hold great significance for Alan. He took hold of it with a resolute grasp and it remained with him throughout his time in hospital.

'I don't normally go in for this kind of thing,' he whispered to me with a smile. 'But I want to die with this cross in my hand. Mind you, John, it's an empty cross. It's a reminder of the resurrection.' Only a few hours later he crossed the finishing line, holding on, like the marathon runner he was, to meet his risen Lord.

Here is a strange paradox: dying is a terrible mystery, but it is an opportunity for growth. Alan was in many ways an ordinary person, not a superhuman saint. But during those last weeks and months he grew emotionally and internally. While his body was deteriorating, his spirit was growing. Dying is a truly wonderful opportunity for personal growth.

The challenges of dying well

What are the fears, challenges, tests and temptations that the dying face? The medieval *Ars moriendi* documents highlighted five temptations, and offered the corresponding virtue to meet each one:

1. the temptation of doubt and the virtue of faith;
2. the temptation of despair and the virtue of hope;
3. the temptation of impatience and the virtue of love;
4. the temptation of pride and the virtue of humility;
5. the temptation of greed and the virtue of letting go.

To the five ancient temptations I would add two modern ones that twenty-first-century believers are prone to:

6. the temptation of denial of death and the virtue of acceptance;
7. the temptation of self-reliance and the virtue of dependence.

So here are seven temptations or tests to which the dying believer may be exposed. Of course, not every person is vulnerable to all seven. But perhaps it is helpful to treat this as a form of checklist. Where are my particular weaknesses and vulnerabilities? And what are the specific remedies that I need to focus on as I approach my own dying?

1. The temptation of doubt and the virtue of faith

In the original *Ars moriendi* documents, the temptation to doubt was illustrated by demons whispering suggestions such as 'Hell is prepared for you', 'Do as the pagans do' or simply 'Kill yourself'.[1] In one manuscript, a demon holds a scroll with a list of accusations based upon the dying person's life. Another demon holds up a shroud to prevent the dying man from seeing the figures of God the Father and God the Son, who are present in the room.

Then, as now, dying brought a fundamental temptation for some to question the reality of the Christian faith and the genuineness of the salvation that trust in Christ brings.

In my experience, many Christian believers do not seem to experience this unnerving temptation to doubt as death approaches. They are granted a sense of confidence and hope that sustains them in their last days. But some believers, even those who have lived and served for many years with obvious and robust faith, struggle at the end with deep doubts, insecurities and fears. Perhaps one of the reasons why we find it hard to talk about our own death is because we find it hard to be honest about our doubts and fears. There may be a sense of shame in admitting to our loved ones or those who provide spiritual care that we are struggling with doubt.

Sometimes the issue is whether God exists at all and whether the entire Christian faith is based on fantasy. Is it really possible that Jesus rose from the dead? Sometimes the question is not so much about the existence of God as the goodness of God. Is it possible that he really cares about me, with my tiny, irrelevant life which is coming to an end in a world of 7 billion people that is just one in a galaxy of 100 million stars? Can it be true that I am genuinely forgiven for the evil that still haunts my memory and my conscience?

Responses to doubt

The first response to the temptation of doubt is honesty: honesty with God, honesty with myself and honesty with my loved ones.

Dietrich Bonhoeffer, imprisoned by the Nazis and facing execution, struggled with his own questions and doubts, which he expressed in his famous poem 'Who Am I?' But the poem ends with an expression of quiet faith: 'Whoever I am, Thou knowest, O God, I am thine!'

> Who am I? They often tell me
> I stepped from my cell's confinement
> Calmly, cheerfully, firmly,
> Like a Squire from his country house.
>
> Who am I? They often tell me
> I used to speak to my warders
> Freely and friendly and clearly,
> As though it were mine to command.
>
> Who am I? They also tell me
> I bore the days of misfortune
> Equably, smilingly, proudly,
> like one accustomed to win.

Am I then really that which other men tell of?
Or am I only what I myself know of myself?
Restless and longing and sick, like a bird in a cage,
Struggling for breath, as though hands were compressing
    my throat,
Yearning for colors, for flowers, for the voices of birds,
Thirsting for words of kindness, for neighborliness,
Tossing in expectations of great events,
Powerlessly trembling for friends at an infinite distance,
Weary and empty at praying, at thinking, at making,
Faint, and ready to say farewell to it all.

Who am I? This or the Other?
Am I one person today and tomorrow another?
Am I both at once? A hypocrite before others,
And before myself a contemptible woebegone weakling?
Or is something within me still like a beaten army
Fleeing in disorder from victory already achieved?

Who am I? They mock me, these lonely questions of mine.
Whoever I am, Thou knowest, O God, I am thine![2]

C. S. Lewis struggled with terrifying doubts about God's goodness following the death of his wife, Joy Davidman. She had been dying of cancer when they first got married, but then, unbelievably and apparently in response to Lewis's prayers, she had recovered. They had spent a blissful period together. But when the cancer returned and Joy died, Lewis was plunged into profound grief. He wrote down his experiences in *A Grief Observed*, which he initially published anonymously.

When you are happy, so happy that you have no sense of needing Him . . . if you remember and turn to Him with gratitude and praise, you will be – or so it feels – welcomed with open arms. But go to Him when your need is desperate, when all other help is vain, and what do you find? A door slammed in your face, and a sound of bolting and double bolting on the inside. After that, silence. You may as well turn away. The longer you wait, the more emphatic the silence will become. There are no lights in the windows. . . . What can this mean? Why is He so present a commander in our time of prosperity and so very absent a help in time of trouble? . . . Not that I am (I think) in much danger of ceasing to believe in God. The real danger is of coming to believe such dreadful things about Him. The conclusion I dread is not 'So there's no God at all', but 'So this is what God's really like. Deceive yourself no longer.' . . .

What chokes every prayer and every hope is the memory of all the prayers [Joy] and I offered and all the false hopes we had. Not hopes raised merely by our own wishful thinking; hopes encouraged, even forced upon us, by false diagnoses . . . by strange remissions . . . Step by step we were 'led up the garden path'. Time after time, when He seemed most gracious He was really preparing the next torture.

What we learn from Lewis is the value of being honest – painfully honest, of expressing the reality of our doubts and questions. Towards the end of the short book of essays, Lewis finds that his fears about the goodness and presence of God are subsiding:

When I lay these questions before God, I get no answer. But a rather special sort of 'No answer'. It is not the locked door. It is more like a silent, certainly not uncompassionate, gaze. As though He shook His head not in refusal but waiving the question. Like 'Peace, child; you don't understand.' . . . Heaven will solve our problems, but not, I think, by showing us subtle reconciliations between all our apparently contradictory notions. The notions will all be knocked from under our feet. We shall see that there never was any problem.[3]

So the first response to doubt is honesty – with myself and with others. The second is the recognition that most Christian believers struggle with doubt at some time or other, and that this painful experience can lead to a deeper and more honest trust in God and his goodness.

Faith in God is not about fixing our problems. As author Margaret Spufford wrote, 'The trust one has to develop in God lies far deeper, in the knowledge that he will be present in the deepest waters, in the most acute pain, and in some appreciation of his will to transform things.'[4]

Andrew Drain was a young surgeon who was dying of leukaemia. He had prayed that God would heal him of the disease, but it seemed that this was not to be. Despite the crushing of all his hopes, Andrew was able to find acceptance and faith during his terminal illness. In his book *Code Red* he wrote, '[R]ather than pray for the weight to be lifted from our shoulders, sometimes we should just pray for stronger shoulders.'[5]

So how should we respond if we find faith difficult and are besieged by doubts? Allen Verhey puts it like this:

A bold Christian affirmation is that because faith in Christ is true and fears no question or challenge, doubt can be a stepping stone to a tougher, deeper faith. In this sense, as George MacDonald asserted, a believer 'may be haunted with doubts and only grow thereby in faith. Doubts are the messengers of the Living One to the honest. They are the first knock at our door of things that are not yet, but have yet to be, understood.'[6]

If we find that we are beset by doubts, it may be right to ask others to exercise faith on our behalf. I may not be able to pray, but I may be able to say 'Amen, yes, I agree' to another's prayer on my behalf. The apostle James did not say that if someone was ill, that person should exercise faith all alone. Instead, he said, 'Is anyone among you sick? Let him call for the elders of the church, and let them pray over him, anointing him with oil in the name of the Lord' (James 5:14). James instructs the suffering patient to take the initiative by calling out for spiritual support and help from the local church community. It is important, then, that we think in advance about whom we could call out to for help if we become besieged by doubts or fears.

Global author and pastor John Stott used to say that, for him, the 'brand image' of a Christian was a figure kneeling at the communion rail, holding out cupped hands to receive communion. This is what it means to be a follower of Christ. ' "Take, eat; this is my body." And he took a cup, and when he had given thanks he gave it to them, saying, "Drink of it, all of you, for this is my blood of the covenant, which is poured out for many for the forgiveness of sins' (Matthew 26:26–28). Jesus offers this precious meal to each of us, but we cannot just be spectators. We do not need to suppress every doubt or question in our minds or generate an extraordinary amount of faith. We just need to stretch out our hands, both metaphorically and literally, and receive what is being offered us.

Since the time of the early church, participation in the Lord's Supper, the Eucharist, has played a special role in the spiritual practices of those who wished to die well. Priests and pastors have taken the bread and the wine to homes, hospital wards and hospices so that those who were close to death could take part in this simple but wonderful act.

Cicely Saunders, the inspiring founder of the modern palliative care movement whom we met earlier, was able to design a hospice in South London. She placed the chapel at the centre of the building, so that every patient in the hospice, however sick, could be pushed in his or her bed into the chapel to take part in the daily round of services, and, if desired, to receive the Eucharist.

And of course, celebration of the Lord's Supper points not only backwards in time to the sacrifice of Christ on the cross. As we receive this precious gift and eat and drink, we are also pointing forwards beyond the grave towards the coming again of Christ and to our participation in the wedding celebration feast of the Lamb. As the apostle Paul said, 'As often as you eat this bread and drink the cup, you proclaim the Lord's death until he comes' (1 Corinthians 11:26).

So, as we approach the ends of our lives on earth, physical participation in the Lord's Supper represents a simple but profoundly significant acknowledgment of our utter dependence on Christ, and of our willingness to receive his saving presence and grace in our lives. But in a metaphorical sense we have to continue holding out our hands and receiving Christ every day of our lives right to the end; it is food for the journey.

2. The temptation of despair and the virtue of hope

In the *Ars moriendi* documents, despair was often illustrated by demons who taunted the dying person with accusations of sin and failure. One illustration shows a demon pointing at a dying woman and accusing her of adultery. Another shows a demon pointing to a destitute beggar as evidence of avarice and selfishness. A third shows a demon holding up a long scroll listing all the sins of the dying person and saying – in a terrible

parody of the words 'Ecce homo' ('Behold the man!') said about
Jesus – 'Ecce peccata tua', 'Behold your sins!' Part of the subtlety
of the accusations is that the demons quote Scripture to
demonstrate the righteousness of God, the seriousness of the
individual sins and failures, and the impending judgment.
'Your situation is hopeless; there is no escape.'

If faith is loss of belief and trust, despair is the loss of hope.
Nothing can improve the situation. Everything is hopeless.
For the person who is facing death, despair is often mingled
with regret: 'If only I had spent more time with my children';
'If only I hadn't allowed my marriage to fail'; 'Why did I waste
my life?'; 'If only I could start all over again.'

To older Christian believers, despair can take on a different
form: 'Why doesn't God take me home? I don't want to live
any more. I've prayed and prayed for God to take me, but he
doesn't answer.' John Dunlop tells the story of Louise, a lady
who had spent fifty years as a missionary taking the gospel to
remote villages. At the age of seventy-five she had to retire
to the USA on health grounds. Louise decided that it was her
time to die, and that she would simply go to bed till the Lord
took her home. John says,

> I tried to tell her that her decision was premature, but she would
> not listen. She had an awesome hope in heaven, but it did not
> prepare her to use the life the Lord had given her on earth. She
> died two years after giving up.[7]

I too have met older Christian believers who have given in
to despair about their lives on earth. Their only prayer is that
God would take them, and their only question is why they are
still alive. I have tried gently to suggest that, if God has not
taken them yet, perhaps it is because they have more to do on
this earth, and perhaps more to learn.

Responses to despair

Just as with doubt, the first step in responding to the temptation of despair is honesty. I have to be honest with myself about the reality of these feelings of hopelessness, regret and despair. But then I have to be honest with my trusted loved ones and companions as well. Instead of maintaining a façade of confidence and faith, it is better to share those feelings. Of course, doing so may be excruciatingly painful. There may be only one or two special people whom we trust enough to say these things to. But putting these emotions into words is often the first step towards recognizing and acknowledging them.

If I have lost all hope, I need others who will encourage and remind me of the realities of the Christian faith. And I need reminding that these temptations, which seem so real and threatening, come ultimately from the Evil One, who is described in the New Testament as the 'accuser of [the] brothers' (Revelation 12:10) and the 'father of lies' (John 8:44).

In one of the *Ars moriendi* images, an angel visits a dying man and encourages him by pointing to figures from the Scriptures who repented and received forgiveness. There is Mary Magdalene, who found forgiveness for her sins; there is the dying thief on the cross; there is Peter, who was forgiven his lies and treachery; and above all there is the Lamb himself, the one who died to bring forgiveness to all who repent.

The medieval writers frequently emphasized the importance of meditating on the figure of Christ on the cross. In a well-known fifteenth-century English text called *The Book of the Craft of Dying* the author quotes the invitation of St Bernard:

What man is he that should not be ravished and drawn to hope and have full confidence in God, and he take heed diligently of the disposition of Christ's body in the cross. Take heed and see: His head is inclined to salve thee; His mouth to kiss thee; His arms spread to embrace thee; His hands pierced to give thee; His side opened to love thee; His body all stretched to give all of Himself to thee. Therefore no man should despair of forgiveness, but fully have hope and confidence in God. . . .[8]

To modern Protestant ears this may sound strange and discomforting, but Christian believers through the ages have meditated on, and prayed to, the suffering Saviour on the cross as they have faced their own deaths. Here is profound mystery.

But there seems to be a deeper mystery than merely being an external observer of Christ's sufferings on the cross. The apostle Paul summed up his own personal hope in these words: '. . . that I may know him and the power of his resurrection, and may *share his sufferings*, becoming *like him in his death*' (Philippians 3:10, emphasis added). In some indescribable way we can have the privilege of entering into and identifying with the sufferings of Christ on the cross. Of course, we cannot compare our own sufferings with the sufferings of Christ. But there is a deep spiritual mystery that Paul's words point to, and perhaps only those who have suffered are able to catch a glimpse of it.

William Cowper was a brilliant poet with a deep personal faith in Christ – but he struggled all his life with episodes of intense despair and depression. At times he was besieged by suicidal thoughts and made several attempts to take his own life. Only the patient, steadfast and practical love of his friends saved him from suicide. And yet out of the devastating experiences of despair and hopelessness came profound moments of insight and faith that were turned into words that still resonate centuries later:

God moves in a mysterious way
His wonders to perform;
He plants his footsteps in the sea,
And rides upon the storm.

Ye fearful saints, fresh courage take;
The clouds ye so much dread
Are big with mercy, and shall break
In blessings on your head.

His purposes will ripen fast,
Unfolding every hour;
The bud may have a bitter taste,
But sweet will be the flower.[9]

G. K. Chesterton once wrote that there were two sins against Christian hope: the sin of presumption and the sin of despair.[10] Presumption is not compatible with Christian hope because it blithely assumes that everything will go well. There will be no problems, no struggle, no testing, no suffering. God will ensure that we pass effortlessly through this life and into his presence – just have faith. This may be attractive, but it is a fantasy. It is not genuine Christian hope, which, above all, is grounded in truth and reality.

But despair is an equal and opposite sin which is also not compatible with Christian hope. Despair says, 'Nothing and nobody can help the current situation'; 'There is nothing to cling on to'; 'There can be no dawning of the light.'

Bishop J. C. Ryle linked the opposites of presumption and despair to the two thieves who were crucified with Christ: 'One thief was saved that no sinner might despair, but only one, that no sinner might presume.'[11]

Instead of the sins of presumption and despair, we are called to practise the *discipline* of Christian hope. The following words were found written on the walls of a cellar in Germany at the end of the Second World War:

I believe in the sun even when it is not shining
I believe in love even when I feel it not
I believe in God even when he is silent.[12]

3. The temptation of impatience and the virtue of love

The third temptation is described in the medieval documents as 'impatience', but a better modern word might actually be 'selfishness'. In the picture, the dying man overturns a table to which his daughter is bringing food, and kicks a visitor in frustration and anger. His wife makes excuses for him, saying, 'See what suffering he endures!', but the picture makes plain that the dying man has succumbed to demonic temptation.

Of course, it is important to emphasize that not every person facing death is tested by every temptation! Nonetheless, there are some who find that they are driven by pain, suffering or loss to respond with annoyance and selfishness. Our normally patient selves are goaded beyond endurance. We can be surprised by our own childish petulance or grumpiness. We find ourselves lashing out at those we love and those who are trying to help. We respond to those who visit with a litany of complaints.

At one level, these feelings and responses are 'only natural'. There may be medical reasons for irritability and aggressive behaviour, such as the effect of disease or oxygen deprivation on brain function. It may be helpful to get experienced professional assessment and advice. But the *Ars moriendi* texts help us to see that there may be a deeper spiritual temptation behind this behaviour: the temptation to focus only on ourselves and our needs to the exclusion of all others.

Responses to impatience (or selfishness)

The healthiest response to our selfishness is to remind ourselves of the needs of others. In that great hymn to *agape* love in 1 Corinthians 13, the apostle reminds us that 'Love is patient and kind . . . It does not insist on its own way; it is not irritable or resentful . . . Love bears all things, believes all things, hopes all things, endures all things' (13:4–5, 7).

Agape love, as described by the apostle Paul, is, above all, the character of the Lord Jesus, reflected in all his actions and in the way that he died. As the soldiers drove the nails through his hands and feet, he prayed for their forgiveness, and in his suffering he took time to remember his mother and to ensure that she would be provided for.

Cheryl Dickow reflected on the selfless love of her sister-in-law Yvonne, who was dying of colon cancer:

[By sharing the experience with those closest to him or her], the person in need of care is allowing the potential caregiver(s) to become mercy and love to another human being. . . .

For the past 18 months, I've watched as family and friends have ministered to Yvonne and can so clearly see how both Yvonne was blessed but . . . how each caregiver was blessed, as well. . . .

The greatest act of selfless love is when one person chooses to share his or her own death with others. When one person is willing to count out the minutes at the hands of another, completely relying on the love and care that can be given but also becoming Love to the caregiver. Not in words or in deeds but in being an instrument.[13]

4. The temptation of pride and the virtue of humility

The *Ars moriendi* texts warn us that, even if we have evaded the temptations of disbelief, despair and selfishness, we are still not safe. There is a subtler but more evil temptation waiting for us: that of spiritual pride. In one of the medieval illustrations one demon offers the dying man a crown and two others hold out a scroll with the words: 'You have persevered in patience.' Another demon utters the words: 'Exalt yourself.'

This temptation seems so much more reasonable than the previous attacks. Surely I can justifiably be a little proud of my perseverance, my patience and the way I am coping so well with these struggles! But in the medieval period, perhaps more so than today, pride – especially spiritual pride – was recognized as a great and subtle evil.

Allen Verhey writes of this temptation:

> Pride gets in the way of dying well. Pride tends to keep suffering and sickness and death at bay. Pride pretends to have no need of either the grace of God or the grace of another human being. It refuses to acknowledge neediness, and it is therefore no good at gratitude. Life frequently has a way of bringing down those who exalt themselves, but if life does not do it, dying will. . . .[14]

Responses to pride

The *Ars moriendi* manuscripts remind us that, if the forces of evil cannot get us through despair and disbelief, they may yet get us through pride and self-reliance. But the medieval documents also point to the remedy. One angel appears to the dying man with the admonition 'Humble yourself', and another reminds him of the punishment that awaits those who rely on themselves, even those who are outwardly religious.

There is a painful and almost brutal honesty in these ancient pictures. It might be our natural tendency to excuse some degree of self-congratulation or self-centredness in those who are facing the reality of death. Certainly, in popular thinking, holding on to the anthem 'My Way' might seem to be a way of coping with forthcoming extinction. Humility is not exactly a popular or widely honoured concept in today's celebrity culture. But medieval believers took much more seriously the injunction of the apostle Peter to 'Humble yourselves, therefore, under the mighty hand of God so that at the proper time he may exalt you' (1 Peter 5:6).

Of course, as many others have emphasized, true humility is not pretending that we are less than we genuinely are. True humility is about being real. Mother Teresa wrote, 'If you are humble nothing will touch you, neither praise nor disgrace, because you know what you are.'[15] The essence of humility is acknowledging the reality of our human condition: that everything we are and everything we have achieved is because of the gift and grace of God. That is true when we are fit and healthy, and it is true when we are on our deathbeds.

5. The temptation of greed and the virtue of letting go

The last of the medieval temptations is that of avarice, or greed. In the illustrations, demons remind a dying man of his many possessions and ask him how he can let these go. They point to his friends and his family and remind him of the pleasures of his earthly life. How can he abandon all the good things of this life? Instead, he should cling on in desperation to the earthly possessions, experiences and relationships he has loved for so long.

This is a temptation for those Christian believers whose hearts are set too firmly in the here and now. Life is good.

I do not feel ready to leave just now. There are so many more things I could do, more goods I could purchase, more pleasures to experience, more places to visit. There are many unfulfilled dreams on my 'bucket list'. If this was a temptation in the medieval period, how much more is it a temptation for those of us who have experienced the benefits and pleasures of our materialistic and hedonistic culture!

In C. S. Lewis's *Screwtape Letters*, the senior devil Screwtape reflects on the diabolical possibilities that come from the tendency of older Christian believers to form growing attachments to this world:

> You will notice that the young are generally less unwilling to die than the middle-aged and the old. The truth is that the Enemy, having oddly destined these mere animals to life in His own eternal world, has guarded them pretty effectively from the danger of feeling at home anywhere else. That is why we must often wish long life to our patients; seventy years is not a day too much for the difficult task of unravelling their souls from Heaven and building up a firm attachment to the earth.[16]

Greed for ever-more experiences and more pleasure seems to be the primary motivation behind the current drive towards using sophisticated science and technology to extend human longevity to 120, 150 or 200 years. When confronted with the temptation of greed, how hard it is for many of us moderns to accept the virtue of letting go.

For those who have served Christ for many years, greed may not be for material pleasures and experiences. Instead, there may be a more subtle greed to carry on serving, to be there for other people, to teach, instruct, witness to Christ and encourage others. We define ourselves by our Christian service and by our willingness to be available for those who need us. We are not ready to go because there is so much more to do.

Responses to greed

So how can we develop the Christian virtue of letting go? In the *Ars moriendi* picture, the dying man is encouraged to look at godly examples of biblical characters who let go. There is Mary, the mother of Jesus, who let go of her own son. There is Christ, who surrendered his glory in order to be born in human form and who gave his life as the Good Shepherd for his sheep. There are the martyrs, who gave their lives for others.

We see a beautiful example of letting go in the Gospel story of Simeon. Luke tells us that this elderly figure was a 'righteous and devout [man who was] waiting for the consolation of Israel' (Luke 2:25). He had been given a deep conviction by the Holy Spirit that he would not see death before he had seen the Lord's Anointed One. Moved by the Spirit, he was drawn to the temple just at the moment when Mary and Joseph brought their baby in to be blessed according to the Hebraic law. Simeon took the baby into his arms and said,

> Sovereign Lord, as you have promised,
> > you may now dismiss your servant in peace.
> For my eyes have seen your salvation.
>
> (2:29–30 NIV)

His prayer (in the Latin words *Nunc dimittis*) became part of the evening liturgy of the Christian church from the fourth century down to the present day.

Theologian Timothy O'Malley writes,

> As I prepare to sleep every night, I practice Simeon's own readiness to die as one who has encountered 'the light of the nations'.

In this way, to pray the Nunc Dimittis is a counter-cultural performance in which each day the Christian practices the art of dying. This is not the death of the philosopher, who acknowledges the brevity of life, and seeks to attune the passions to this inescapable reality. Rather, it is the death of those who have seen the very source of salvation made manifest in the weakness of the infant Son. The death of those who have desired to see God enact the definitive plan of salvation and now abide in a world in which God's glory has taken flesh.[17]

T. S. Eliot's poem 'A Song for Simeon' captures the same theme:

Let the Infant, the still unspeaking and unspoken Word,
Grant Israel's consolation
To one who has eighty years and no to-morrow.[18]

Simeon had seen only a newborn baby, but with eyes of faith he could see something else: that God's glorious plans and purposes of salvation were underway and that they were utterly secure and unbreakable; this is, as Timothy O'Malley put it, 'a world in which God's glory has taken flesh'. When we are overtaken by that conviction, it is *safe* to let go.

John Dunlop writes,

To the extent that we can understand and experience God's love for us, develop a longing for God, and find ourselves increasingly satisfied with him more than all other things in this life, we will be prepared to die and to enter his presence. We will find what we have longed for and more. But if we are grasping on to the things of this earth, we will never be fulfilled.[19]

In his evocative short story 'Leaf by Niggle', J. R. R. Tolkien tells a parable of a painter called Niggle. He was not a very successful painter. But he had a vision of a great tree with glimpses of forest and a mountain in the background, and he knew he had to paint it. He was continually distracted from his painting, running errands for other people, and the painting was only part-way completed when, very unexpectedly, Niggle was told he must go on a long journey, clearly a symbol of death. '"There now!" said the Inspector [a mysterious angelic character who supervises Niggle's departure]. "You'll have to go; but it's a bad way to start on your journey, leaving your jobs undone. Still, we can at least make some use of this canvas now."'

Eventually, after a long period of waiting, Niggle arrived in a spring meadow, and as he explored this wonderful new land he discovered a tree:

> Before him stood the Tree, his Tree, finished. . . . All the leaves he had ever laboured at were there, as he had imagined them rather than as he had made them; and there were others that had only budded in his mind, and many that might have budded, if only he had had time. . . . [T]he Forest was there too, opening out on either side, and marching away into the distance. The Mountains were glimmering far away.

Back in his home town the community had largely forgotten Niggle and his unfinished painting. Most of the painting had crumbled, but one beautiful leaf remained. It was framed and placed in the Town Museum with the title: 'Leaf: by Niggle', but eventually the museum burnt down and Niggle and his leaf were forgotten in the old country. But the real Tree remained, and Niggle was able to enjoy it in all its glory and to get to work in the wonderful land, planting new trees, plants and hedges.[20]

Tolkien's parable points to the way that, in God's wonderful redemptive purposes, all the unfinished tasks and chaos of our lives may be redeemed, renewed and fulfilled by his grace. We can let go, knowing that his love and grace are greater than our plans.

When my friend Alan Toogood found that he had terminal cancer, he found it hard to let go. His natural response to any obstacle was: 'I'm going to beat this.' He had made a commitment to care for his disabled wife, Sheila, to the end, and it hurt him that he could not fulfil his promise. 'I wanted to be there for your mum,' he told his daughters, Karen and Alison. Afterwards they told me, 'It was as though he had written the script in advance but it didn't work out.' For Alan, letting go meant that he had to release his hold, to transfer the care of Sheila to his daughters. 'It was the hardest thing for him, but slowly he was able to pass over the baton.'

During his final hours in hospital it was very important that Alan could express his love for Sheila. He asked his daughters to get his wedding ring so that he could die with it on his finger. And he dictated a final letter to Sheila, which he and the family have given me permission to share:

> To my dear Sheila:
> I have loved you for more than 57 years. I will always love you because you are a treasure to me. Our eternity is assured *because of Jesus*. If I'm there first, my joy will be to welcome you with open arms because our love remains an everlasting love. *Thank you for everything.* The Lord bless you and keep you and make his face to ever shine upon you. Ever yours. Your Alan

Sheila was also ill, in another hospital, but she was able to come for a precious last visit. Once she had visited, it was as though Alan had been given permission to go. His daughters remained with him for the last hours, holding his hands. He opened his eyes and said, 'You're both lovely, you are.'

'Dad, it's OK, we've got Mum; go and be with your Lord and Saviour.' Minutes later, he gently and peacefully slipped away.

Karen and Alison Toogood have talked about the impact their father's death has had:

> It was faith-affirming to witness someone die like that.

> It's hard to explain, but there's a lot of hope.

> Before I would have dreaded and feared the death of my father. But when it happened, it was so . . . positive. God took him very gently.

> Throughout our lives we learnt to do various tasks by quietly standing alongside Dad and watching him do them. And now he was teaching us how to die.

> I came away from it with such a positive view of dying. God was in control the whole time. As you put your foot into the darkness, God puts a stepping stone there.

So those were the five medieval temptations – doubt, despair, impatience, pride and greed. To those five I have added two additional temptations to which people today seem to be particularly prone: first, the denial of death and, second, self-reliance.

6. The temptation of denial of death and the virtue of acceptance

As we noted earlier, the modern technological world of healthcare offers the dying a temptation that was not available to medieval believers. In their world, death was everywhere.

It could strike at any moment, whatever precautions you took. Everybody knew that the plague was sweeping through Europe and that those who were infected had little chance of survival.

But modern medicine can offer us the idea – the delusion – that death can be kept at bay indefinitely. We grasp at stories of amazing new treatments for cancer, gene therapy, regenerative medicine, transplant surgery, research breakthroughs and wonder drugs. Of course, we know in theory that death cannot be held back for ever, but we prefer to focus on the positive. Disease is an enemy to be fought, and we will keep on fighting. We buy into the battle imagery of modern medicine and we vow never to give up.

Author Rob Moll quotes a funeral director in Wheaton, Illinois, USA, who said that the most common Bible verse that families put on funeral announcements or read at services is: 'I have fought the good fight' (2 Timothy 4:7). 'Except they are not talking about spiritual things. . . . They mean this person tried every medical option to stay alive.'[21] Christian physician John Dunlop says, 'Medicine is . . . good, but not when we are shaking our fists in God's face and saying "No, I'm not going to die yet. I'm trusting technology to pull me through."'[22]

As John Dunlop says, there are many aspects of modern medical technology that are admirable. We noted earlier that the medical struggle is witnessing to the goodness of the creation and of bodily life with all its glories and its vulnerabilities. It is demonstrating that death is an enemy that is worth fighting with all our perseverance and courage, in advance of death's ultimate destruction in the new creation. But preoccupation with the medical battle also represents a temptation. It may become an unhealthy way of evading reality, and a refusal to face the fact that, though the medical struggle will go on elsewhere, our own life is coming to an end.

One of the unhealthy consequences is that a degree of pretence enters into the relationship between the dying person and his or her relatives and carers. I have to pretend that I believe I am going to get better, although deep inside I have a terrible fear that this is not true. However, I have to maintain an upbeat and confident demeanour in order not to hurt my loved ones. At the same time, my loved ones feel an emotional pressure to maintain the appearance of confidence and optimism, in order not to hurt me. At its worst, the end result of all this complicated emotional game-playing is that the precious last hours and days of life – which ought to be a time of deep honesty and openness between the dying person and his or her closest friends and family – are instead turned into a charade of pretence and collusion.

Unfortunately, this complicated form of game-playing is not unusual at the end of life, and it is something that I have witnessed on a number of occasions. Sometimes doctors find themselves caught up in the charade. Although doctors may wish to explain to patients that they are dying and that medical treatment is not going to be able to extend life, some relatives state point-blank that they do not want their loved one to be informed 'because he/she will lose all hope'. Even though the doctor tries to explain the value of openness and honesty in facing death, the relatives are adamant that the pretence of recovery must be maintained.

Of course, it is true that we all need to have a source of hope, in order to face each day. Without hope, living becomes a form of hell. As a doctor caring for many dying patients and for the parents of disabled children and critically ill babies, I know that to talk to suffering people in a way that annihilates all hope is cruel and destructive. Maintaining and feeding hope is essential. But the critical question, of course, is where our hope for the future is being placed.

If our hope is in the power of medical technology to overcome every obstacle, we are doomed to ultimate disappointment. What is worse, this kind of hope may stand in the way of godly acceptance of God's will for the last phase of our life, impeding the possibility of strengthening or 'completing' our relationships in a healthy and faithful way.

So where should we place our hope as we come to the end of our lives? This is a theme that recurs throughout this book, and it has several aspects. In the near term, we have to choose to place our hope in the loving presence of God, who has promised to walk with us through every phase of our life, including through the valley of the shadow of death:

> Even though I walk through the valley
> > of the shadow of death,
> > I will fear no evil,
> for you are with me;
> > your rod and your staff,
> > they comfort me.
> (Psalm 23:4)

Then we place our hope in God's redemptive power and grace, which is able to take the pain, suffering and evil of dying and turn it into blessing and healing. We remind ourselves of the opportunities that we looked at in the previous chapter: of internal growth, and of healing, building, celebrating and completing relationships. Here is something to hope in. God has more to do in us and, through us, in the lives of other people.

I think it is also quite appropriate to place our hope in the love and faithfulness of other people: relatives and loved ones,

Christian pastors and those who will pray, and the professionals who are there to give their expertise and wisdom. Of course, our hope and trust in people are not the same as our hope in the Saviour. But they are a source of encouragement nevertheless. It is important to remember that we will not die alone. There are people who love us and who will walk with us to the end.

Finally, and ultimately, as believers we place our hope in the covenant faithfulness of the Father, who has known and loved us from before the foundation of the world, who has called us into existence and called us to himself, and who holds us utterly secure and unshakeable in his knowledge and steadfast love. He has promised to take us to himself and to raise us up with a new body in the new heaven and the new earth. Yes, there are solid grounds for hope – both in this world and in the next. (We will focus in greater detail on the hope of resurrection in chapter 7.)

Sometimes a spiritual element enters the denial of death. I am praying and exercising faith that God is going to heal me. Whatever the medical evidence suggests, I must remain steadfast in my faith and I must not allow any doubts about the reality of the coming healing to enter in. I will refuse to acknowledge 'faithless talk' about the apparent deterioration of my condition, and instead claim the healing that I desperately believe and hope is coming. Within this way of thinking it would be an act of doubt and a lack of faith to agree to stop active medical treatment. Instead, I must insist on every possible medical intervention as a demonstration of my steadfast faith in God's healing power!

There is little doubt that this way of thinking lies behind the paradoxical evidence we looked at earlier from studies of religious believers with a terminal condition in the USA. This showed that such believers were more likely to die in an intensive care unit, receiving full life support to the very end, than those who stated that they did not have religious beliefs. It seems sadly ironic that the effect of Christian convictions about miraculous healing can lead unintentionally to death in an intensive care unit, sedated or anaesthetized, surrounded by machinery and cared for by anonymous professionals – above all, tragically isolated from loved ones and all the possible sources of human and spiritual consolation.

Responses to denial of death

So how can we resist the modern temptation of death-denial, and especially its subtle spiritual overtones?

The Christian virtue of *acceptance* is not a passive resignation in the face of overwhelming forces. Rather, it is a positive act of trust in the goodness and the grace of God. In his helpful book *A Thorn in the Flesh*, Pablo Martinez distinguishes between a godly Christian acceptance and other forms of resignation.[23]

On the one hand, there is a stoical or fatalistic *resignation* to suffering and death. This is based on a deep sense of human impotence in the face of the overwhelming forces of nature. 'There's no alternative, so one might at least accept the inevitable.' As Pablo Martinez points out, this attitude tends to breed both passivity and bitterness.

> *The Christian virtue of* acceptance . . . *is a positive act of trust in the goodness and the grace of God.*

An alternative and popular approach to suffering and death is to adopt a form of detachment or disconnection from painful reality. 'I won't allow this to affect me. I'll enter into an inner zone and ignore any unpleasant experiences and thoughts.' This response is similar to the teaching of Eastern religions that all suffering is an illusion and that the correct response, through constant training in meditation and inwardness, is to achieve a mental state that transcends suffering. The goal is to achieve an inner *detachment* from the experience of suffering.

But godly Christian acceptance is not based on resignation or detachment. Instead, it is founded on a living and personal *trust* in the goodness and the grace of God. We see this kind of godly acceptance modelled frequently in the lives of God's people as related in the Scriptures.

The Old Testament story of Job gives a striking example of godly acceptance. The text says that, when he received the catastrophic news that his children had died and his possessions were destroyed,

> Job arose and tore his robe and shaved his head and fell on the ground and worshipped. And he said, 'Naked I came from my mother's womb, and naked shall I return. The LORD gave and the LORD has taken away; blessed be the name of the LORD.'
> (Job 1:20–21)

Job does not minimize the terrible losses that he has experienced. He tears his robe and shaves his head in a public sign of grief and mourning. But he finds the grace to express his trust in the goodness and faithfulness of the Lord, using the name Yahweh, the covenant name, despite the apparently capricious and meaningless tragedy of his children's death.

Above all, we see acceptance modelled in Christ's struggle in the Garden of Gethsemane as he faced the awful reality of his impending crucifixion and all that it would mean. For Christ, this was the time of his ultimate test. But there is not a hint of stoical resignation or mystical detachment. Instead, he cries out, 'Father, if you are willing, remove this cup from me' (Luke 22:42). Luke records that, in Jesus' agony, 'his sweat

became like great drops of blood falling down to the ground'
(22:44). Mark tells us that Jesus was 'greatly distressed and
troubled' (Mark 14:33). Matthew writes that Jesus said, 'My
soul is very sorrowful, even to death; remain here, and watch
with me' (Matthew 26:38).

The writer to the Hebrews describes the emotional intensity
of Jesus' struggle in prayer with his Father: 'Jesus offered up
prayers and supplications, with loud cries and tears, to him
who was able to save him from death, and he was heard
because of his reverence' (Hebrews 5:7). The final outcome
of this painful struggle were those searing words: 'nevertheless, not as I will, but as you will' (Matthew 26:39). It is
profoundly significant that Mark records that Jesus prayed,
'*Abba, Father*, all things are possible for you. Remove this cup
from me. Yet not what I will, but what you will' (Mark 14:36,
emphasis added). His prayer was the prayer of a loving and
trusting Son: 'Abba, Father; Father, I trust you; Father, I want
what you want.'

The struggle that we face is not to be compared with
what Christ experienced in Gethsemane, but here we find
a powerful model of godly acceptance. It is a model that
Christian believers over the centuries have turned to as they
approached their own deaths.

7. The temptation of self-reliance and the virtue of dependence

The final temptation of self-reliance is one that had little
appeal for medieval believers. They lived in a dangerous and
chaotic world in which – except for a very small group of the
rich and powerful – any illusion that you were capable of
controlling your own destiny was ridiculous. But we live in a
very different world, one which offers us the illusion of

control. We prize autonomy (from *auto-nomos*, 'self-rule'). We wish to lead our own lives and make our own choices. We do not wish to depend on others, as children do. We are adults. We want to make our own way in the world.

There is no doubt that the motivation for individual autonomy is driving the demand for the legalization of assisted suicide and euthanasia across the world. Autonomy is the principle behind patient choice, the touchstone of modern healthcare. In the UK, autonomy is enshrined in the Patient Charter, the NHS Constitution, the Mental Capacity Act and General Medical Council guidelines for doctors. It is the patient who should be at the centre, choosing and controlling what treatment should be given. And, since we have the right to make choices about every other aspect of our medical treatment, why do we not have the right of self-rule when it comes to precisely when and how we die? (This is an argument that I have addressed in greater detail in *Right to Die?*, the companion volume to this book.)

The emphasis on individual choice as the ultimate expression of my identity and self-worth highlights a deep fear: the fear of dependence. Dependence is seen as threatening and dehumanizing, precisely because it threatens my sense of identity, my sense that my life is worth living. Many people who have lived their lives as an expression of self-determination and self-reliance are horrified by the prospect that their manner of death might represent an abdication of these principles. As surgeon Atul Gawande puts it, 'Our reverence for independence takes no account of the reality of what happens in life: sooner or later independence will become impossible.'[24]

The modern celebration of choice, control and self-reliance can be traced to its roots in the European Enlightenment of the eighteenth century. It was part of the Enlightenment rejection of all forms of divine and political authority, and the creation of the idea of the autonomous individual.

But the idea of self-reliance is common among Christian believers too. It is often expressed as a fear of 'being a burden' to others. 'I'm very happy to care for other people and to look after their needs. But if I ever start to become a burden to other people, if I need to be cared for and looked after, then I would rather go to heaven. I'll pray that God will take me.' Superficially, this sounds altruistic and spiritually minded. But the truth is that this attitude is a long way from an authentic Christian understanding of what it means to be human, and of the human nature that has been given to us by our Creator.

Responses to self-reliance

I did not choose to be a human being, to take on this form of physical embodiment, this frailty and these limitations. And I was not born as an isolated individual. I came into the world embedded into a network of relations I did not choose, with a mother and father, grandparents, siblings, aunts and uncles, friends and carers. You and I came into the world as helpless beings, utterly dependent on the love and care of people we did not choose. We go through a phase in our lives when other people depend on us. We protect them, care for them, feed them, pay for them. And then most of us will end our physical lives utterly dependent on the love and care of others. We will need other people to feed us, protect us and care for us. This is not a terrible, degrading, inhuman reality; it is part of the design. It is a part of the narrative of a human life.

A daughter who had cared for her mother in her final illness put it like this:

> When I think about it now, caring for Mom wasn't all that
> different from how I cared for my kids when they were babies –

or how Mom cared for me when I was little. I hope I helped make her last moments as love-filled as she made my first moments after I had entered the world.[25]

I cannot count the number of times I have heard mature Christian believers (who ought to know better) say, 'I don't want to be a burden.' Yet the reality is that this is part of what it means to belong to a family or to a community. Theologian Gilbert Meilaender wrote an article entitled 'I Want to Burden My Loved Ones' in which he said, 'Is this not in large measure what it means to belong to a family: to burden each other – and to find, almost miraculously, that others are willing, even happy, to carry such burdens?'[26] This is true for a human family, and it is also true for the Christian family, the local church.

Paul commanded the Galatians, as members of the Christian family, to 'Bear one another's burdens, and so fulfil the law of Christ' (Galatians 6:2). To be called into a family is to be called to share the burdens of the life that God has given us, the burdens that come from our creation out of dust. The life of a family, including the local Christian church family, should be one of 'mutual burdensomeness'.

Ira Byock, a palliative care physician, writes how, when the dying give their loved ones the privilege to serve, they are helping them to complete the relationship and also aiding them in their future grieving process.[27] John Dunlop continues the same theme:

There is an essential humility that makes us willing to be served. Christians should have learned at the time of their salvation that they can do nothing to save themselves, but are totally dependent on God. Throughout life a desire for self-sufficiency can impair spiritual growth. At the end of life, it is good to be less self-sufficient and trust God more fully.[28]

There is a profound sense in which Jesus Christ himself entered into the experience of dependence. He was born as a pathetic, fragile baby. He could do nothing for himself. He needed human arms to cuddle him, clothe him, clean him and keep him warm. He needed a human mother to feed him.

And, at the end of his earthly life, Christ allowed himself to become dependent again. In his book *The Stature of Waiting* William Vanstone points out that there is a significant moment in the Gospel narratives where there is a marked reversal in the way in which Jesus is depicted. In the first part of the Gospel narratives, Jesus is the active and initiating subject. He calls, he speaks, he appoints, he heals, he travels. The narrative emphasizes the dynamic and active character of his life and ministry. But from the point at which he is betrayed by Judas and handed over to the authorities, the narrative changes. Jesus is still at the very centre of the story, but now he is no longer the active subject. He is there as the recipient, the object of other people's actions. As Jesus stands, silent and motionless, other characters emerge from the wings to carry the story forward. 'They took him'; 'They led him'; 'They dressed him'; 'They crucified him.'

Vanstone points out that, in Mark's Gospel, from the time when Christ is handed over until the time of his death, he appears to *do* nothing whatever. On many occasions he refuses to speak; he gives no answer. When he does speak, his words are disregarded or seem ineffective. Following the handing over, he is no longer the one who does; he becomes the one who is done to. In the first part of the narrative, Jesus is the one who has *freedom* to proclaim his Father's truth and to demonstrate his Father's compassion. But following the sudden reversal in the Garden of Gethsemane, his unfettered freedom is transformed into bondage.

When Jesus stands before Pilate, one of the questions Pilate puts to him is: 'Do you not know that I have authority to release you and authority to crucify you?' (John 19:10). Previously, Christ had exercised complete authority in his ministry – authority to judge, authority to heal – but now Pilate claims and exercises authority over him. Instead of refuting and overcoming Pilate's power with a blast of spiritual authority, Jesus accepts that Pilate's claim of authority over him is real. Yes, Pilate, you do have authority of life and death over me, and I have been given over into your hands – but 'You would have no authority over me at all unless it had been given you from above' (John 19:10).

William Vanstone makes a further point that the common term 'passion' used in connection with Christ is derived from the Greek *pascho*, which means literally 'to be done to'. Vanstone writes,

> To be faithful to the Gospel record we must reserve the expression 'the passion of Jesus' for that distinct phase of his life into which he entered when he was handed over to wait upon and receive the decision and deed of men, to become an object in their hands.

Yet the Gospel writers emphasize that, paradoxically, the glory of God is revealed most powerfully in Christ in his passion. His glory is revealed in dependence and 'passivity'. In John's Gospel, when the band of soldiers comes to take him, we find these words:

> Then Jesus, knowing all that would happen to him, came forward and said to them, 'Whom do you seek?' They

answered him, 'Jesus of Nazareth.' Jesus said to them,
'I am he [*Ego eimi*].' . . . When Jesus said to them, 'I am he
[*Ego eimi*]', they drew back and fell to the ground.
(John 18:4–6)

Vanstone comments,

> In John's Gospel, alone among the Gospels, there is no
> transfiguration of Jesus upon a hill top – no moment when
> chosen witnesses have a brief glimpse, a brief visual perception
> of who he really is and are overwhelmed by what they perceive.
> In John's Gospel the transfiguration of Jesus is, so to speak,
> transferred to the Garden of Gethsemane at the moment when
> he is handed over, and those who are overwhelmed by it and
> bear witness to it by falling to the ground are the men who have
> come to take him into their hands. It is as Jesus is handed over,
> as he enters into passion, that the ultimate dimension of the
> divine glory becomes manifest in him and evident to men.
>
> It is not through the teaching of Jesus nor through his mighty
> works that the deepest dimension of the divine glory is disclosed in
> Jesus . . . it is through the fact that, of his own will, he places himself
> in men's hands and becomes exposed to whatever they will do.[29]

Through this strange and wonderful paradox we can catch
glimpses of a deep truth. To be dependent on others is not
degrading and dehumanizing, for in the painful reality of
dependence we experience a tiny reflection of what God, out
of love, chose for himself. Christ's divine status and dignity
were in no way impaired by his dependence. In fact, in
that very dependence his divine glory was displayed to all,
including to those who wished him harm.

Of course, this does not mean that allowing oneself to
become dependent is easy or straightforward. In my own

limited experience of serious illness I have discovered how hard it is to depend on others for care and love. It is painful to watch others whom you love struggle with the load of caring for you. If I can say it reverently, I have no doubt that it was not easy for Christ himself. The Lord of total power and authority chose to make himself utterly dependent. And the people to whom he handed himself over were not loving carers, but vicious, brutal men. But he went this way before us to show us the mystery of glory revealed in dependence.

> *In the painful reality of dependence we experience a tiny reflection of what God, out of love, chose for himself.*

Summary of the seven temptations

So here are the seven temptations, the seven types of testing to which dying people may be subjected: doubt, despair, impatience, pride, greed, denial of death, and self-reliance. It is a pretty intimidating list. Of course, as I mentioned earlier, not every person is vulnerable to all seven. Thank God that none of us is vulnerable to all these types of testing. But I do believe it is helpful to treat this as a kind of checklist.

Immediately before they take off, pilots complete a last checklist: 'Runway heading – set; flaps – take-off setting; fuel – sufficient; engine readings – normal; take-off clearance – received . . .' Perhaps, as believers in Christ, we might find it helpful to go through our checklist before the ultimate take-off! Where are my particular weaknesses and vulnerabilities, and what are the specific remedies that I need to focus on as I approach the runway?

Now we turn to challenges of a different nature: communicating honestly with loved ones and with healthcare professionals as the end of life approaches.

5

Communicating honestly

An official UK government report on end-of-life care offers a helpful framework for patients with a terminal illness, describing timeframes as death approaches (see diagram).

THE END OF LIFE At risk of dying in 6–12 months, but may live for years	MONTHS 2–9 months	SHORT WEEKS 1–8 weeks	LAST DAYS 2–14 days	THE DYING PHASE LAST HOURS 0–48 hours
DISEASE(S) RELENTLESS Progression is less reversible Treatment benefits are waning	CHANGE UNDERWAY Benefit of treatment less evident Harms of treatment less tolerable	RECOVERY LESS LIKELY The risk of death is rising	DYING BEGINS Deterioration is weekly/daily	ACTIVELY DYING The body is shutting down The person is letting go

Framework of timeframes as death approaches
(Crown Copyright 2013)[1]

At the first stage there is evidence that the underlying disease is progressing and that treatments are increasingly ineffective. At this point, death is likely within six to twelve months, although some patients may live for years. At the second stage there are further changes in the progression of the underlying disease, and the harms caused by treatment become less tolerable. Death is likely within two to nine months. At the third stage, the disease progresses further, the risk of death is rising, and death is likely within one to eight weeks. At the fourth stage, deterioration is noticeable on a daily basis, and death is likely within two to fourteen days. In medical terminology, the phase of 'dying' has begun. At the final stage, which may last up to forty-eight hours or so, the body is shutting down and the person is letting go. Medically, this is described as the person 'actively dying'.

In reality, every person and situation is different, and this framework provides only approximate guidelines about time-scales. Sometimes a person who appears to be close to death may improve unexpectedly and the risk of death will recede by weeks or months. Other people with chronic disease may appear to be close to death for many months. Nonetheless, this framework is helpful in enabling patients and carers to understand the normal progression of disease processes at the end of life.

As we face the reality that our life on earth is coming to an end, there are important topics that may need to be discussed both with those who are closest to us and with healthcare professionals.

What symptoms am I likely to suffer? How can these be alleviated?

Talking to professionals in advance can provide reassurance about the range of treatments available to ensure that un-pleasant symptoms are well controlled. Being honest about our fears and anxieties can help the healthcare team to ensure that our particular concerns are addressed and that suitable treatments and aids are available. It also helps if we can talk about our fears with our loved ones. Many people are understandably concerned about the possibility that they will suffer excruciating pain as they approach the end. But, in reality, provided there is good medical and nursing care, physical pain can usually be controlled very effectively and either abolished or at least greatly reduced.

Some people are anxious that doctors and nurses will use opioid medicines such as morphine in a deliberate attempt to shorten their lives, or that they will become addicted to the medication. These anxieties have been fed by media reports and by recognized concerns about the actions of inexperienced health staff. Such concerns have been heightened by the misleading argument that morphine is a highly dangerous and lethal poison, and that, when doctors give morphine at the end of life, they are intending to kill but covering their tracks.

This is dangerous misinformation. Morphine and other opioids are very effective painkillers, but in fact they are not dangerous lethal drugs unless used in massive overdose. The misinformation about morphine is dangerous because patients may refuse to take adequate amounts of opioids for pain relief, fearing that doctors are secretly trying to end their lives. In reality, there is good scientific evidence that, when used appropriately in terminal illness, morphine and other opioids do not accelerate death; in fact, paradoxically, they sometimes extend life by alleviating pain and distress. Opioids do not normally cause marked sleepiness, and medications can nearly always be adjusted to provide good pain relief without excessive sedation.[2]

Other people are anxious about embarrassing problems such as incontinence, or the possibility of becoming confused or 'losing my mind'. Again, it is helpful to verbalize such concerns and ask the professionals about what treatments might be available.

Should I carry on receiving treatment for my condition in the hope that it might prolong my life? Or would it be better to stop?

It is important to understand that stopping a medical treatment that is intended to treat a disease is not the same as euthanasia, intentional killing or suicide. All medical treatments are intended to help the patient, to do good. But, at the same time, all medical treatments carry the risk of complications. They can bring burdens, and can end up causing unintentional damage and harm. At the heart of all decision-making about medical treatments is the balancing of the likely benefits against the burdens and risks. Good medical care has always included the withholding or withdrawing of treatment that is excessively burdensome compared with its likely benefits. This means that it is very important to try to weigh up the likely benefits and burdens of any medical treatments at the end of life, something that should be undertaken collaboratively with doctors and relatives.

What does this mean in practice? Suppose I know that I am dying with advanced cancer that has spread throughout my body. The physicians have told me that there is now no possibility of a cure and that I am likely to die within the next three months or so. Should I carry on receiving anti-cancer treatment, chemotherapy, right up to the end? The doctors think that the treatment may extend my life by, at most, a few weeks or months. The truth is that anti-cancer treatment may be very unpleasant, leading to frequent hospital visits, tests and expense, and the effect of the treatment on my body may make me feel continually nauseous, fatigued and exhausted. Is this worth the benefits that the treatment may bring – that is, increasing my chances of a few extra weeks or months of survival? The answer is: 'It all depends.' In different circumstances, and with different individuals, the balance between burdens and benefits will change.

For some people, the extra weeks that invasive treatment can bring may be of profound significance and richness, an opportunity for all kinds of 'unfinished business' to be completed: the fulfilment of a long-cherished ambition, or the chance to enjoy the presence of children or intimate friends. In other situations, the opportunity of living for a few extra weeks may seem to bring little benefit compared with the burdens, upset and complications of invasive treatment. It is all too possible for medical treatments to transform the last weeks of life from a time of peaceful preparation for death into a miserable, wretched experience. Sometimes we need the courage to say 'no' to the possibilities of burdensome medical treatment – not out of cowardice or suicidal intent, but out of a desire to die faithfully, in a manner consistent with our Christian faith.

Health professionals often refer to the limitations of treatment or 'ceilings of care'. As a person's disease progresses, the likelihood of benefiting from invasive treatment decreases, and the likelihood of side effects and complications increases. In discussion with the patient, and with his or her agreement, professionals may then decide that there should be a 'ceiling of care' beyond which they will not go, in order to reduce the harms to the patient caused by overtreatment. A person with advanced disease may decide against being admitted to hospital or being transferred to an intensive care unit, choosing rather to receive palliative care and symptom control instead of the

> *Sometimes we need the courage to say 'no' to the possibilities of burdensome medical treatment.*

additional burdens imposed by invasive, uncomfortable and medically futile treatment.

Should I agree to a 'Do Not Attempt Cardiopulmonary Resuscitation' order?

A very practical issue which frequently causes distress and confusion is that of a 'Do Not Attempt Cardiopulmonary Resuscitation' order (DNACPR; sometimes known informally as a 'Do Not Resuscitate' order). This is for any patient who is at risk of a cardiac or respiratory arrest.

A degree of incomprehension and conflict between the health professionals and the patient often seems to arise on this difficult issue. On the one hand, the professionals see a DNACPR order as an act of practical compassion, because it avoids the possibility that the patient will be subject to the indignity of intensive cardiopulmonary resuscitation, including cardiac massage and electric shocks, when there is in fact no chance of successfully restoring life. In most hospitals, if there is no DNACPR order signed by a senior doctor, health professionals perceive a duty to commence resuscitation at the point of death. (In reality, this seems to be a misperception: there is no legal or moral duty on health professionals to commence resuscitation if it can bring no benefit.)

On the other hand, patients may interpret the acceptance of a DNACPR order as an implicit agreement, first, that their own lives have no value and that they want to die, and, second, that they are to be abandoned by the health professionals who will concentrate on other patients who are getting better. Understandably, many patients (and relatives, if they are involved) are offended by these perceptions and do not wish to agree to a DNACPR order, as it seems to be an inappropriate act of despair. As a result, much time and emotional energy are spent on repeated discussions and debates about the DNACPR order, which, frankly, is of minor significance compared with other questions about the care that will be provided in the final days and hours of life.

Dr Kathy Myers, an experienced palliative care physician, told me,

> The way I explain DNACPR to patients is to say that CPR is a particular specialist treatment for people who appear to have died suddenly from a cardiac or respiratory arrest, and that it is not a treatment for 'natural' death from the consequences of the disease they have. I also explain that it can be traumatic, and that their chances of surviving it would be extremely slim, given their particular illness, and that if they are at home or in a hospice, it would mean they would have to be sent to hospital in an ambulance.

This was an issue for my friend Alan Toogood as he approached the last days of his life; again, he and his daughters gave me their permission to write about his experience. As we saw in the previous chapter, Alan found it very difficult to accept that his life was drawing to a close. He had made a commitment to care for his disabled wife, Sheila, to the end, and it hurt him that he could not fulfil his promise. When his cancer came back and he was readmitted to hospital at a terminal stage of the illness, the hospital staff repeatedly asked him to give his agreement to a DNACPR order.

Alan was hoping upon hope that he would get better so that he could care for Sheila again. For him, to agree to the order seemed to be giving up on his duty and his commitment to Sheila. He was also worried that to agree not to be resuscitated would represent a lack of faith. In some sense, it felt as though he was giving up on his Lord. I had the opportunity to discuss this with him at length in the hospital. I tried to explain that the hospital staff felt that, without a DNACPR order, the law said that he should be resuscitated. Alan said, with a smile, 'That's all very well, John, but I am not concerned about *the law*; I'm concerned about *the Lord*.'

Alan remained adamant that he would not agree to the order. His condition improved somewhat and he was able to leave hospital. But when he was readmitted, shortly before his death, he changed his mind and gave his agreement to the DNACPR order. 'I think I've been a bit stubborn,' he told his daughters. Alan was able to die peacefully and with dignity in hospital, with his daughters by his side, and the hospital staff were reassured that no emergency resuscitation needed to be carried out when his death occurred.

Where would I like to die?

Although many people die in hospital, most people, when asked, say that they would prefer to die at home or in a hospice. If this is the case for you, it is important to try to plan ahead so that appropriate arrangements can be made. Community palliative care teams exist to provide excellent end-of-life care in a variety of settings. With planning and resourcefulness, many people who would otherwise die in hospital could be cared for in their own homes, and they could end their lives in a familiar setting. From my own perspective, dying at home, where possible, seems much more desirable than dying in the alien and institutionalized setting of a hospital. But it can sometimes be difficult to arrange this at very short notice. There is a series of practical questions that need to be addressed. Who will provide nursing care over each twenty-four-hour period? Who will provide the medical support and ensure that necessary treatments are available in the home? What aids will be required in the home? Will it be necessary to obtain a special 'hospital' bed? And so on.

It is important to plan ahead when it comes to palliative care, even if it is not certain that death will come soon. This is sometimes called 'twin-track planning': in other words, we make plans simultaneously for two different outcomes. On the one hand, we make some plans assuming that the disease will respond to treatment and that we have weeks or longer ahead of us. At the same time, we make other plans for palliative care in case it turns out that my condition deteriorates and I discover that I have only days left.

The UK government has recommended a framework called 'Advance Care Planning' as a means of improving care for people nearing the end of life and for enabling better planning and provision of care, to help them live well and die well in the place and manner of their choosing. (Further information about end-of-life care is provided in Appendix 1, and resources are listed in the Notes section at the end of the book.[3])

Who will support me spiritually?

Good palliative care aims to support the whole person and to address all forms of distress – physical, psychological, relational and spiritual. If we are Christian believers, it is vitally important to know that we will receive pastoral support and care from friends at church or from a trusted pastor or elder. We are not alone in the Christian family, and we are called to bear one another's burdens and to be there for one another, particularly at the end of life. If there are particular individuals you would like to support you spiritually at the end, it may be helpful to express your wishes in advance and let them know.

Earlier I referred to my friend Stuart, the young man who died of advanced cancer. He had been coming to All Souls Church, Langham Place, London, for some years but had never had the chance of a personal conversation with John Stott, who at that time was Rector Emeritus. When he was close to the end, Stuart asked Rico Tice, the then newly appointed curate, if it would be possible for him to meet John Stott for a brief conversation. In response, John welcomed Stuart to his bachelor flat close by the church, and they not only enjoyed a long conversation and prayed together, but John took him out for a meal and spent the evening with him. There is spiritual and personal support available for us if only we will ask for it.

We are called to bear one another's burdens and to be there for one another, particularly at the end of life.

We have looked at the five temptations of the *Ars moriendi* and two modern-day temptations. We have also looked at some of the practical questions that modern healthcare raises around the process of dying. But, after illustrating the temptations and their corresponding virtues, the medieval writers turned to Christ himself as the model of one who died well, a model from whom we could learn. That is the theme of our next chapter.

6

Learning from the example of Jesus

I approach this chapter with a deep sense of inadequacy. I am conscious that we are standing on holy ground. And we must be extremely careful about drawing any superficial comparisons between the unique death of Jesus Christ and our own experiences. Jesus is the Son of the living God, and his death on the cross was utterly unique. His suffering and death stand at the centre of history.

Everything that had happened from creation past – the fall, the history of salvation, the whole story of the cosmos – focused to a single point in space and time. A few short hours at Golgotha, in the strange and wonderful drama on the cross, was the very central point of history. And, in the death of Christ, death itself was defeated.

O death, where is your victory?
O death, where is your sting?
(1 Corinthians 15:55)

So how could we dare to make any comparison between his

momentous death, a death that occurred 'once for all', and our own?

And yet, for two thousand years, dying Christian believers have looked to the death of Christ. They have reflected and meditated on his dying as an example to learn from, a model of what it means to die well. In the passage that Philippa Taylor quoted in chapter 3 the writer to the Hebrews instructs us to

> run with endurance the race that is set before us, looking to Jesus, the founder and perfecter of our faith, who for the joy that was set before him endured the cross, despising the shame, and is seated at the right hand of the throne of God.
> (Hebrews 12:1–2)

The apostle Peter tells us that 'Christ also suffered for you, leaving you an example, so that you might follow in his steps' (1 Peter 2:21).

In order, then, to learn from the example of Jesus, we first need to turn to Jesus' words spoken in the Garden of Gethsemane just before he was crucified – words to which we have already referred.

'Abba, Father, all things are possible for you. Remove this cup from me. Yet not what I will, but what you will' (Mark 14:36)

> And they went to a place called Gethsemane. And he said to his disciples, 'Sit here while I pray.' And he took with him Peter and James and John, and began to be greatly distressed and troubled. And he said to them, 'My soul is very sorrowful, even to death. Remain here and watch.' And going a little farther, he fell on the ground and prayed that, if it were possible, the hour might pass

from him. And he said, 'Abba, Father, all things are possible
for you. Remove this cup from me. Yet not what I will, but
what you will.'
(Mark 14:32–36)

The disciples did not understand what they saw, but they
sensed the mystery and the holiness of the hour. We may
understand a little more in the light of what was to come, but
there is still much that we cannot comprehend. We are
spectators as the Son and the Father commune – not in quiet
tranquillity, but in agony.

'Gethsemane' means 'olive press'. The garden was a grove
of ancient olive trees on the sides of the hill in Jerusalem
called the Mount of Olives. Its name indicates that it was the
place where olives were crushed under a large millstone so
that the precious oil could drip out. It seems that it was a
regular place of prayer for Jesus and the disciples. No doubt
he understood the symbolic significance of the name long
before they did. This was the place where he would start to
experience the crushing weight of the evil of the world, so
that the precious oil of sacrifice and healing could flow out.

'Abba, Father,' he said, 'all things are possible for you. Take
this cup from me. Yet not what I will, but what you will.' As
we noted in an earlier chapter, the word 'Abba', widely used
in the language of the time, is an intimate word, the word of
a child in the arms of his or her father. It could have been the
first word a child uttered, an expression of intimacy, openness
and trust. In his moment of agony and sorrow, the Son of
God uses this word to address his Father.

In contrast to many of the great figures of the past who
went to their deaths serenely and courageously, we see that
lonely figure in the olive grove prostrate, sweating, overwhelmed with grief and dread, and begging, if possible, to be

spared the drinking of the cup. In both the wisdom literature and the prophetic writing of the Old Testament, the Lord's 'cup' was a symbol of God's terrible wrath.

It seems that, because Christ shared our humanity fully, like us he needed to be tested, to be trained in obedience. He needed to learn from the experience of the Garden of Gethsemane. The first man, Adam, was tested in a garden and failed – with terrible consequences. The second Adam was also tested in a garden, but he learnt obedience through suffering. The writer to the Hebrews said, 'Jesus offered up prayers and supplications, with loud cries and tears, to him who was able to save him from death, and he was heard because of his reverence' (Hebrews 5:7). God heard his cry and answered it.

We cannot fully understand the horror that Christ contemplated, but Luke records that his anguish as he prayed was such that 'his sweat became like great drops of blood falling down to the ground' (Luke 22:44). In Gethsemane we see sorrow, distress and agony. But we also see the courage of Jesus in the face of the ultimate test that he was undergoing. We see his faith and trust in his Father, and we see his determination to remain faithful to the end.

> He came and found them sleeping, and he said to Peter, 'Simon, are you asleep? Could you not watch one hour? Watch and pray that you may not enter into temptation. The spirit indeed is willing, but the flesh is weak.'
> (Mark 14:37–38)

I find it profoundly touching that he, the Son of God, asked his friends – weak, confused and exhausted as they were – to be with him at the time of his suffering. 'Remain here and watch.' Even Christ did not want to face death alone. He wanted his closest friends to be there with him. Dying is not a journey to be taken alone. It is to be taken with those who are closest to us, with our heart companions and loved ones, with those who will stay and watch and pray.

The struggle we face is not to be compared with what Christ experienced in Gethsemane. Because he has experienced the agony of sin on our behalf, none of us need face the same abandonment and emptiness. But, as we saw earlier in chapter 4 on the temptations of dying, Gethsemane is a powerful model of faith, trust and godly acceptance for us as we approach our own departing.

> *Dying is not a journey to be taken alone. It is to be taken with . . . those who will stay and watch and pray.*

I referred in chapter 3 to Katie Bryson, the talented young artist who discovered at the age of nearly twenty-seven years that the cancer of her childhood had returned in an incurable and progressive form and whose story is told in *Dying Without Fear*. Here is a poem she wrote following the diagnosis:

Wake me up from this nightmare God!
Surely it's just a dream
Why, why, why is there a killer in my neck?
Why wait for now?
Why did it come when life was good with art, painting and beads?
Such highlights, joys and achievements, real inner treasure
and values.
Friendships, blessings and sparkles, beauties turned
so upside down,
Still there but, oh so different!
Life experience isn't always an easy package.
Wake me up from this nightmare God!

Surely it's still only a dream.
But if somehow it brings you more glory
May your will be done.[1]

Katie was able to take on to her lips the words that Jesus prayed: 'May your will be done.'

We do not need to try to create in ourselves an intense peak of godly fervour. Instead, in a sense, we have to allow the Spirit to pray within us. Wonderfully and mysteriously, we can allow the Spirit of Jesus within us to pray the same prayer of intimacy, trust and acceptance that Christ prayed to his Father: 'Abba, Father, may your will be done.'

'Father, forgive them, for they know not what they do' (Luke 23:34)

'Who can forgive sins but God alone?' asked the Pharisees (Luke 5:21), and they were right. In this word spoken from the cross, Jesus the Son of God is pronouncing cosmic forgiveness. Many commentators have pointed out the ironies in Luke's account of the crucifixion. Those who scoff at Jesus are in fact speaking the truth (Luke 23:35–39). Pilate, the cynic, places an inscription on the cross which does in reality proclaim the truth about Christ's kingship. And Jesus, condemned by an unjust judge, prays that his righteous Father will forgive those who are justly condemned.

So it is clear that Luke means to stress the uniqueness of Christ's death and the universal significance of this word of forgiveness from the cross. Yet it is very striking that Luke later records that Stephen, the first Christian martyr, used the same words as he was dying: 'falling to his knees he cried out with a loud voice, "Lord, do not hold this sin against them"' (Acts 7:60). Luke clearly wanted his readers to draw a connection between the manner in which the Christian martyrs died and the example they had seen in Christ.

The readiness to forgive is a mark of dying well. The forgiveness that Christ brings and the forgiving attitude he models break the cycle of grievance, bitterness and retaliation. Forgiveness restores broken relationships and brings joy where there was previously acrimony and resentment, as we saw in chapter 3 in the story of Mary who experienced the grace of forgiveness just days before she died. So, as we approach our own dying, we have a once-in-a-lifetime opportunity to learn more of the grace-gift of forgiveness. The words of Paul take on special relevance and urgency: 'Let all bitterness and wrath and anger and clamour and slander be put away from you, along with all malice. Be kind to one another, tender-hearted, *forgiving one another, as God in Christ forgave you*' (Ephesians 4:31–32, emphasis added). When we forgive others, we bear witness to the forgiveness we ourselves have received from Christ.

To die well and in a manner that is faithful to Christ, we cannot be nursing grievances, complaints and grudges. We seek to receive afresh God's grace for ourselves and to be channels of that grace to others. Paradoxically, the dying person may be given a kind of relational authority, both in asking for forgiveness and in offering forgiveness. It is hard to refuse the request of someone who is facing death: 'Please listen to me. There is something I want to say to you . . .'

We die well and faithfully not only by a readiness to forgive, but also by a readiness to ask for forgiveness. We may need to apologize and to make things right. Thanks to the death and resurrection of Christ, we are free to begin again, even as we are dying. We are able to find reconciliation, healing and restoration of relationships that may have been broken for years. Dying well is an opportunity to start again.

'Today you will be with me in Paradise' (Luke 23:43)

> One of the criminals who were hanged railed at him, saying,
> 'Are you not the Christ? Save yourself and us!' But the other
> rebuked him, saying, 'Do you not fear God, since you are under
> the same sentence of condemnation? And we indeed justly, for
> we are receiving the due reward of our deeds; but this man has
> done nothing wrong.' And he said, 'Jesus, remember me when
> you come into your kingdom.' And he said to him, 'Truly, I say
> to you, today you will be with me in Paradise.'
> (Luke 23:39–43)

The two thieves hang alongside the dying Christ, within
inches of him, and see everything – but their reactions are
totally different. One hurls insults and contempt. He is
motivated by despair and bitterness. The other recognizes the
paradoxical reality, sees the ironic notice written by Pilate
placed above the cross – 'This is . . . the King of the Jews' –
and chooses to submit to Christ's kingship: 'Jesus, remember
me when you come into your kingdom.' He is motivated by
faith and hope.

The thief is dying, but he faces a greater and more fearful
reality: what Scripture calls 'the second death'. He recognizes
that he is under a sentence of condemnation. But this is not
just the condemnation of the Roman authorities. He is aware
of his deep spiritual guilt, and he fears not physical death, but
what John Stott called God's 'steady, unrelenting, unremitting,
uncompromising antagonism to evil in all its forms and
manifestations'.[2] His is not just physical pain, it is spiritual
pain. In his desperation, the dying man cries out to the dying
Christ at his side, and he instantly finds forgiveness.

And so an anonymous dying criminal becomes the pattern,
the model, of the Christian believer. 'King Jesus, remember

me.' Christ ignores the insults of the crowd and the contempt of the first thief. He remains silent in front of his accusers, but he responds immediately to the cry for help, a cry of faith: 'Truly, I say to you, today you will be with me in Paradise.' The construction of the Greek puts the emphasis on the words 'today, with me'.

The thief prayed that the Lord would remember him in his coming kingdom, but Christ assured him that, before that very day had passed, he would be with the Saviour. The thief asked to be remembered in a kingdom, but Christ assured him of a place in Paradise. The thief simply asked to be 'remembered', but the Saviour declared that he would be 'with me' – 'today, with me'. In the very place of despair, agony, contempt and blood is a lightning flash of faith, hope and love.

The repentant thief appears in the medieval *Ars moriendi* illustrations as an example of repentance and hope in response to the temptation of despair. He is the most powerful and authentic scriptural model of a true deathbed conversion. His words 'Jesus, remember me' were frequently inscribed on early Christian gravestones.

The dying thief also became a model of what it means to die faithfully despite the horrific circumstances of his execution. Instead of being self-absorbed in misery, suffering and despair, he recognizes the presence of Christ next to him and he reaches out in faith. His prayer is not eloquent or theologically profound – but it comes from the depths of his being. And Jesus' response is immediate and welcoming: 'today, with me in Paradise', a promise not of some distant salvation, but salvation today.

What we learn from this dramatic incident is that Paradise is not far from the deathbed of the one who is prepared to call out in faith. But what exactly is this Paradise? We cannot fully understand it, and this book is not the place to engage with the theological debates and controversies on the issue, but Christ tells us here all we really need to know: it is being 'with me'.

Earlier, Christ had said to his disciples, 'I am going [to my Father's house] to prepare a place for you. And if I go and prepare a place for you, I will come back and take you to be *with me*' (John 14:1–3 NIV, emphasis added). In Matthew's account of the last supper Jesus says, 'I tell you I will not drink again of this fruit of the vine until that day when I drink it new *with you* in my Father's kingdom' (Matthew 26:29, emphasis added).

The writer to the Hebrews said that it was 'for the joy that was set before him' that Christ endured the cross, despising its shame (Hebrews 12:2). Here we get a glimpse of that joy. It is not a solitary joy; it is the joy of being together with his beloved disciples and followers – 'with me'.

'Woman, behold, your son!'; 'Behold, your mother!' (John 19:26–27)

Of all the four Gospel writers, only John notes that Mary the mother of Jesus, together with Mary the wife of Clopas and Mary Magdalene, was standing by the cross, witnessing the suffering of her son (John 19:25). She had had an intimation of this day over thirty years previously in the strange words of Simeon in the temple:

> Simeon blessed them and said to Mary, his mother, 'Behold, this child is appointed for the fall and rising of many in Israel, and for a sign that is opposed (and a sword will pierce through your own soul also), so that thoughts from many hearts may be revealed.'
> (Luke 2:34–35)

Now that word was being fulfilled. As she watches her beloved son in agony on the cross, Mary's innermost being is pierced by that sword of grief, horror and fear. And Jesus, in the midst of his own agony and the jeers and contempt of the crowd, is aware of his mother's anguish. He reaches out in love and compassion: '"Woman, behold, your son!" Then he said to [John] the disciple, "Behold, your mother!"' The words are brief, but they are full of tenderness, gentleness and thoughtfulness. And they were never forgotten. John writes that 'from that hour the disciple took her to his own home'.

John's Gospel, more than the others, points to the pre-existent divinity of Christ and the glory that was revealed in his crucifixion and resurrection. And yet these words recorded by John are remarkably practical and down-to-earth. A dying son is making what provision he can for his mother's care and protection after he has gone.

If we are to die well, we must not allow ourselves to become totally preoccupied with our own needs and concerns. Dying well involves a practical and loving concern for the needs of others. This may involve some kind of spoken or symbolic handing over of responsibilities. As the eldest son, Jesus carried a responsibility to support and protect his mother. Now, moments before his death, he is handing over that responsibility to the person whom he trusts the most, his closest disciple, the one who 'lay on his bosom' (in the literal Greek text of John 13:23). And John would never forget those words, nor the solemn responsibility he had been given.

A crucified hand is open; it can no longer hold or grasp. It must let go.

Formally to hand over responsibilities for others is part of what it means to let go, the virtue of godly acceptance.[3] To use a well-known image, our hands tend to close on to, to grasp, things and people that are dear to us. But a crucified hand is open; it can no longer hold or grasp. It must let go.

'My God, my God, why have you forsaken me?' (Matthew 27:46)

With this saying from the cross we enter the deepest darkness of the dying of Christ – the darkness of abandonment. David Webster has written, 'At the birth of the Son of God there was brightness at midnight; at the death of the Son of God there was darkness at noon.'[4]

When Jesus was betrayed by Judas, he said to the band of officials sent to arrest him, 'When I was with you day after day in the temple, you did not lay hands on me. But this is your hour, and the power of darkness' (Luke 22:53). This is your hour: the hour for every imaginable force of evil, malevolence and hatred to be let loose, when God's light seems to be obliterated; the hour when darkness rules.

We see that Jesus was not only rejected by the Jews as a blasphemer and executed by the Romans as a rebel, but that he was also condemned and abandoned by his Father. The One to whom he had cried 'Abba, Father' now turned his back.

> How great the pain of searing loss –
> The Father turns His face away,
> As wounds which mar the Chosen One
> Bring many sons to glory.[5]

In that awful experience that divided God from God, we recognize that both Father and Son suffered the cost of their loving surrender. The Son suffered dying and abandonment; the Father suffered the death of, and separation from, the Son.

We glimpse the infinite grief of the Father's heart in the abandonment of his Son. As Jürgen Moltmann put it, 'The Fatherlessness of the Son is matched by the Sonlessness of the Father.'[6]

We are not able to penetrate this deepest mystery of the cross; we can only, like Mary and the other women, stand and watch. Surely in this respect Christ's death was utterly unique. He suffered total abandonment from God, so that those who believe in him might be reconciled and brought close. There is a sense in which, because Jesus spoke those terrible words 'My God, my God, why have you forsaken me?', we who put our trust in him are saved from ever having to articulate them.

But there is another sense in which we may be called to take those words on to our lips. In his hour of darkness Jesus turned to the Hebrew Psalms and quoted the first line of Psalm 22, a psalm which epitomizes the tradition of godly lament within the Old Testament. Of course, Jesus knew the Psalms and he knew Psalm 22, 'a psalm of David'. How strange it must have been for Jesus to have read it and to have known that, although David had written these words hundreds of years earlier, they were his words as well. On the cross, during those hours of darkness, he took David's words on to his lips. God himself, in the person of Jesus, took those words of lament and made them his own. God was lamenting to God.

Both Jesus and the Gospel writers knew that, although Psalm 22 starts with that terrible cry of dereliction, 'My God, my God, why have you forsaken me?', it does not end there. There is a clear trajectory through the thirty-one verses.

The first eight verses repeat the sense of utter abandonment by God, but from verse 9 there is a change in tone:

Yet you are he who took me from the womb;
>you made me trust you at my mother's breasts.
On you was I cast from my birth,
>and from my mother's womb you have been my God.
(22:9–10)

Verses 12–21 have descriptions of the besieging enemies and of the physical weakness and distress that the psalmist experiences. But from verse 22 to the end of the psalm there are confident expressions of faith and hope:

I will tell of your name to my brothers . . .
For he has not despised or abhorred
>the affliction of the afflicted,
and he has not hidden his face from him.
(22:22, 24)

And the psalm ends with praise and a confident declaration of God's completed work of salvation, which extends to the whole world and to the cosmic future:

Posterity shall serve him;
>it shall be told of the Lord to the coming generation;
they shall come and proclaim his righteousness to a people
>>yet unborn,
>that he has done it.
(22:30–31)

Godly lament is not an expression of faithlessness or despair; it is an expression of faith and trust in God and resistance to evil. The words of lament that we find in the Old Testament Scriptures provide faithful language with which we can bring our pain to God. As John Swinton puts it,

'Lament is a way of reframing suffering in the light of the hope and promises of God.'[7]

Dying well may involve godly lament. We should not attempt to disguise or suppress the feelings of loss, pain and abandonment that may sweep over us. If we are being faithful to Christ and to his example as a dying man, we may take the words of lament we find in the Old Testament and make them our own:

> *'Lament is a way of reframing suffering in the light of the hope and promises of God.'*

Why, O LORD, do you stand far away?
 Why do you hide yourself in times of trouble?
(Psalm 10:1)

How long, O LORD? Will you forget me for ever?
 How long will you hide your face from me?
(Psalm 13:1)

Deep calls to deep
 at the roar of your waterfalls;
all your breakers and your waves
 have gone over me.
(Psalm 42:7)

In words that we have already looked at, the writer to the Hebrews tells us that Jesus 'offered up prayers and supplications, with loud cries and tears, to him who was able to save him from death, *and he was heard because of his reverence*' (Hebrews 5:7, emphasis added). Christ was heard by his Father. Those terrible words of lament did not fall on deaf ears. The words of Psalm 22 were vindicated:

He has not despised or abhorred
    the affliction of the afflicted,
and he has not hidden his face from him.
(22:24)

By faith, we can say the same for our own feeble laments. God did not finally forsake and abandon his dying Son, and, if we take the same words of lament on to our lips as death approaches, he will not abandon us either.

Because Christ experienced that ultimate abandonment, we need never fear the darkness. Allen Verhey writes on Psalm 22:

If and when in the face of death we make this psalm our own, we may be sure that we are not and will not be abandoned. We may be sure that Christ is with us. He knows the dark recesses of our caverns of gloom; he was there first. Into whatever pit of loneliness we fall, Christ can find us. . . . We may cry out to God in anger and in hope, in anguish and in faith, joining the sad complaint that it is not yet God's good future to a sure confidence in the faithfulness of God. We may lament.[8]

'I am thirsty' (John 19:28 NIV)

Here is a strange paradox: the maker of heaven and earth with parched lips! This is the profound mystery of the incarnation. The Son of God, who upholds the entire cosmos by the word of his power, chooses to make himself utterly and totally dependent on others. He empties himself and enters into the overwhelming experience of human need and human agony. With arms outstretched, he can do nothing for himself. He willingly puts himself at the mercy of his enemies, and he suffers the very human and basic experience of thirst.

Perhaps we can learn from this that there is nothing we can experience physically and emotionally in the process of dying that, in a sense, God himself, in the person of Jesus, has not already experienced. God has experienced humanity from the inside – he knows what it means to be thirsty, weary, fatigued, sleepless and emotionally exhausted. The writer to the Hebrews states, 'For we do not have a high priest who is unable to sympathize with our weaknesses, but one who in every respect has been tempted [tested] as we are, yet without sin' (Hebrews 4:15).

The physical experience of dying seems to be very varied and unpredictable. Many people find that, as death approaches, even though they are eating or drinking very little, they do not seem to experience hunger or thirst. There may be a feeling of peace and even exultation. For others, however, there may be distressing physical symptoms. Thankfully, palliative care doctors and nurses have developed considerable expertise in managing distressing symptoms, and there is no need for anyone to go through the painful experiences that our medieval brothers and sisters underwent.

But dying well may still involve either literal physical thirst or more metaphorical longings that cannot be satisfied so easily. For some people, it seems that dying becomes a testing of their deepest desires.

What is it that you desire above all else? In his book *Learning to Dance*, Michael Mayne reflected on his own approaching death. He saw that many of the fleeting desires of his life had a deeper resonance:

> They all point to home, the place where there is an end to all our searching, and where there is no need to explain, for everything is known. Here on earth there is beauty, but why is it so fleeting? There is joy, but why is it always achingly incomplete?[9]

So, perhaps, as we approach the end of our lives, we are being given an opportunity to test our hearts, to ask what it is that we desire above all else.

It is the thirst for God himself that he longs to strengthen within us, so that he can satisfy those deepest longings in his presence. It seems that his goal is in some sense to detach our focus from the other desires of our hearts and to draw them to himself.

'Whoever drinks of the water that I will give him will never be thirsty again. The water that I will give him will become in him a spring of water welling up to eternal life' (John 4:14). For those who come to Christ there is the promise of an endless spring of living water to quench and drown the deepest longings of our hearts.

And at the very end of the book of Revelation, the water of life reappears, as the Spirit and the Bride look forward to the glorious second coming of Christ. 'The Spirit and the Bride say, "Come." And let the one who hears say, "Come." And let the one who is thirsty come; let the one who desires take the water of life without price' (Revelation 22:17).

'It is finished' (John 19:30)

> When Jesus had received the sour wine, he said, 'It is finished,'
> and he bowed his head and gave up his spirit.
> (John 19:30)

In the Greek text the cry 'It is finished' is the single word *tetelestai*, 'Finished!' The word is derived from *telos*, meaning 'the end', and it is in the perfect tense. I understand that it means literally, 'It has been and for ever will be finished.'

Jesus' work on the cross is completed. The cry is not the whispered acknowledgment of defeat; it is a cry of triumph and accomplishment. He has completed the task that his Father gave him. And he has died well.

What looks from the outside like the defeat of goodness by evil is actually the reverse: evil is being overcome by goodness. Crushed by the ruthless power of Rome, Christ is in fact crushing the serpent's head. The victim is in reality the victor, and the cross is the throne from which Christ rules the world. His death is the death-blow to Satan's kingdom; it is the very process by which death is overcome by life.

Just as the entire history of the cosmos, creation and fall had focused to this single point at Golgotha – to this literal crux of history – now the future opens up and widens towards the resurrection, the coming of the Spirit, the foundation of the redeemed family of believers, and then on towards the new heaven and the new earth and the marriage feast of the Lamb who was killed.

At the end of the book of Revelation the risen and glorified Jesus says again, 'It is done. I am the Alpha and the Omega, the Beginning and the End [the *arche* and the *telos*]. To the thirsty I will give water without cost from the spring of the water of life' (Revelation 21:6 NIV).

Of course, we cannot apply the universal significance of Christ's death to our own. But there is a sense in which, to die well, we too have to be prepared to say, 'It is finished.' Because Christ's cosmic work is completed, our little lives can have an eternal significance. We are given the honour of having a tiny part in the drama. We are bit-players in the cosmic drama of the Lion and the Lamb – a drama that started before the foundation of the world and will last to 'the ages of the ages'. We can try to play our bit-part well and faithfully, and when this phase of our bit-part comes to an end, we can say in faith, hope and love, 'It is finished.'

But, of course, the reality is that our lives are full of brokenness and partially fulfilled achievements. There is the evil we have done and the good we have not done. This is why, in order to die well, there is often work to do. There are relationships that may need strengthening, faith that needs nurturing, final goals or dreams to be fulfilled, the writing down or telling of our life stories to pass on to the next generations, the preparing of ourselves to meet our Lord. We may need the help of our loved ones to decide on the priorities for the days and weeks that remain.

Dying well means being at peace with God and at peace with the most important people in our lives. Then we too can have the courage and faith to take on to our lips those words: 'It is finished.'

'Father, into your hands I commit my spirit!' (Luke 23:46)

In Gethsemane Jesus' prayer had started with 'Abba, Father', the cry of sonship, and at the very end of his work on the cross he cries with a loud voice, 'Father, into your hands I commit my spirit!' The darkness, the agony of abandonment and separation from the Father, is over.

Some commentators have suggested that, even on the cross, Christ could not be killed as we can be killed. In him was life: he was the source, the fount, the origin, of life. How could the life-giver be killed by human hands? As Christ had said of his own life, 'No one takes it from me, but I lay it down of my own accord. I have authority to lay it down, and I have authority to take it up again' (John 10:18). He had voluntarily to relinquish his life into the hands of his Father. His life was not torn from him; he chose to give it back to his Father and, as he died, he became the great life-giver.

The dying prayer of Jesus was taken up as a model by early Christian believers. Stephen, as he was being stoned, called out, 'Lord Jesus, receive my spirit' (Acts 7:59).

Christ's words are also found in Psalm 31:

Into your hand I commit my spirit;
   you have redeemed me, O LORD, faithful God.
(31:5)

The word 'commit' implies giving oneself to the care and protection of another. It is a word of trust and faith. The words were part of the evening prayers spoken by observant Jews at the time of Christ. Perhaps Jesus too had used this prayer many times at the end of the day, knowing that it was a preparation for the hour of his death.

Dying well involves faithful prayer. And the more we have lived with faithful prayer, the more those prayers will be with us as we approach the end. But prayer is not always easy on the deathbed. Some people find that, because of pain, illness or fatigue, it becomes almost impossible to pray. Here is an essential role for those who care for us, our companions on the final journey: if I cannot pray for myself, you must pray for me. If I cannot find words of faith, you must exercise faith on my behalf. If I cannot recall those verses or hymns that meant so much to me, you must retell them. If I have even forgotten who I am and what was most important to me, you can remind me and reassure me.

As we have seen, dying well also involves letting go, a positive act of relinquishment and giving oneself into the Father's hands. Sometimes it seems that dying people need a kind of 'permission' to let go. They cling on to life, to each breath, perhaps out of a sense of duty to others, or a sense that it is 'not safe' to let go. It can be very helpful, when the time is right, for loved ones at the bedside to give this permission verbally.

For Alan Toogood, as we saw earlier, it was concern for the care of his wife and his responsibilities as a husband that remained with him in those last days. But once Sheila his wife had visited, he was able to let go. His daughters spoke words reassuring him that they would look after her, and minutes later he gently and peacefully slipped away.

7

A sure and steadfast hope

Let us step back to the Genesis narrative and look at the Creator's strange and wonderful creation plan. He chose to take his own image, his likeness, and to enshrine it, embody it, in a pathetic, weak, vulnerable and fragile carbon-based life form. He chose to make a first Adam, a being made out of dust (in Hebrew *adamah*), a 'groundling', and designed him to reflect God's wonderful character and being.

It was a strange, remarkable and risky enterprise. And, tragically, it looks as though it has gone hopelessly and catastrophically wrong. Those wonderful and fragile human beings, image-bearers, have become fallen, perverted and contaminated by evil. There is so much wickedness, so much pain, so much distress, so much confusion, so much hatred. Surely the best thing would be to wipe the slate clean and start again? Adam, the groundling, needs to be wiped out of cosmic history, and there needs to be a fresh beginning . . .

But then Jesus, the second Adam, is born as a physical human being, and he too is made out of dust. He develops from a minute speck in a human womb. He is born a helpless baby, grows and learns about the world. He lives in Palestine, experiences the gamut of human emotions and then gives his life on a cross. He is 'dead and buried', in the words of the Nicene Creed. But then, impossibly, inexplicably, wonderfully, he rises physically from the dead.

The Gospel writers go to great lengths to emphasize the physical reality of Christ's resurrected body and its continuity with his old physical body. The narratives are all adamant: *the tomb was empty*. The risen Jesus eats and drinks. He breaks bread. He talks. He prepares a meal. He is touched. He is recognized by his astonished friends. His body even bears the physical scars that were inflicted by the Roman soldiers. There is no room to doubt that there is physical continuity between Jesus' original body and his resurrection body. The same molecules that composed his original body are somehow changed and incorporated into his risen body. His new form of existence is not something utterly alien and different, a completely new kind of reality; it is the same, but different. He is Adam all over again – but different.

It is as though God himself enters our space–time universe and picks up a scoop of dust, of *adamah*, and pulls it back into himself in the incarnation. Christ's body is composed of dust – carbon, phosphorus, trace elements, cells, mitochondria, DNA, the ashes from a burnt-out supernova. But then, by the working of God's resurrection power, those particular atoms are somehow transformed into a new kind of physical reality, a new kind of physics, Physics 2.0 – and the very first mani-festation of this new kind of physics is the resurrection body of Christ.

So the central mystery of the resurrection is that there is both continuity and discontinuity; the risen Christ is the same and yet he is different. It is notable how frequently his disciples and followers fail to recognize him. Mary, who had stared into his face on many occasions, thinks that he is the gardener. The disciples on the Emmaus road listen to an extraordinary Bible lesson at length, and yet fail to work out who this mysterious teacher is. The disciples in the boat fail to recognize him standing not far away on the shore.

Jesus went out of his way to reassure his bewildered disciples that he was the same person. 'Why are you troubled, and why do doubts arise in your hearts? See my hands and my feet, that it is I myself. Touch me, and see' (Luke 24:38–39). The faith and trust in his Father that marked his life from the beginning all the way to the cross is characteristic of the risen Christ too: he is the same person. 'It is I myself' – this is the reassurance on which the Christian hope of resurrection rests. 'Don't be frightened – I am the same person.'

So, in one sense, the resurrection looks back to Jesus' life on earth. But in the same resurrection we also see that the physical man Jesus of Nazareth has been transformed by God's power. His body is now part of a new reality – a future reality that has somehow penetrated backwards into our space–time. The resurrection appearances are encounters with divine power and authority. Humanity is elevated to a place that it has never enjoyed before: the place at God's right hand that belongs to his Son.

In God's mysterious purpose, this is what human beings were always intended to become. This is the ultimate goal of the created order. In Jesus, the second Adam, we see both a perfect human being (what the original Adam was meant to be) and the pioneer, the blueprint, for a new type of humanity, the one in whose likeness a new creation will spring.

As Paul says in 1 Corinthians 15:20, 'Christ has been raised from the dead, the firstfruits of those who have fallen asleep.' The image is from the time of harvest. The 'firstfruits' were the first produce of the harvest, which was offered to God as an acknowledgment that the entire harvest belonged to God. Paul says that Christ's risen body is the 'firstfruits' of the coming harvest. In other words, the resurrection of Jesus is part of the great resurrection that will come at the end of time – but it has come early. Paul's argument in 1 Corinthians 15 insists on a deep connection between the resurrection of Jesus and the final resurrection. It is not possible to believe, trust and rely on Christ's resurrection unless one also believes, trusts and relies on the future resurrection that is integrally related to Christ.

In the resurrection body of Jesus we catch the first glimpse of the new humanity, of *Homo sapiens* mark 2. As Paul writes, 'Just as we have borne the image of the man of dust, we shall also bear the image of the man of heaven' (1 Corinthians 15:49). The image of God inherited from Adam will be fulfilled and transformed into a new and much more glorious image. Yes, we shall still be reflections; we shall still be images. We shall not lose our creaturely dependence. But we shall discover the true likeness that we were always intended to bear, the true identity that we were intended to indwell.

In the physical resurrection of Christ our humanity is both vindicated and transformed. It is all part of the plan, the deep story that started from before the dawn of time, from 'before the foundation of the world', to use the biblical language. Because the story of the cross does not stop on Good Friday; Easter Sunday is to come – in fact, Easter Sunday has already started.

In 1 Corinthians 15, Paul draws out the striking contrasts between the body that is 'sown' and the body that is raised. The body 'is sown' in one form and it 'is raised' in another. Paul is using the analogy of the relationship between the seed and the flower. It is a dramatic image encapsulated in the strange paradox of the seed packet. The contrast between the tiny brown specks of tissue on the inside and the multi-coloured splendour pictured on the outside of the packet is startling. If you had never witnessed the transformation, you might not think it was possible. Yet in those tiny and pathetic fragments of tissue is packed all the information (in the form of DNA) that is required to create the glorious blooms. The two entities, which seem to be so different, share a common hidden identity. The seed is in the process of becoming what it already is.

Paul is saying that it is the same for human beings. Locked inside our weak and decaying, unimpressive bodies is all the information that will go to make our glorious new bodies.

'What is sown is perishable; what is raised is imperishable' (1 Corinthians 15:42)

As we know only too well, our bodies are subject, like the rest of the creation, to decay and futility. It is the cycle of nature, and, according to the natural death movement, the only way to wisdom and to peace is to recognize the inevitability of impending decay and dissolution. But the Christian hope is far more wonderful. The natural cycle of life and death will be broken. Death will be annihilated, swallowed up in life, and therefore our new bodies will be different.

Our resurrection bodies will still be dependent on God for their life. We will still be creatures rather than the creator. But because of God's faithfulness, power and never-changing being, because of the character and dynamism of the life-giving Spirit, our resurrection bodies will not decay and deteriorate. They will be imperishable.

'It is sown in dishonour; it is raised in glory' (1 Corinthians 15:43)

Our current bodies are dishonourable in the sense that they are fragile and pathetic, even comical. Our pitiable bodies do not demonstrate the wonder of the person within. I have frequently experienced this as a doctor when caring for somebody at the end of life whose body has been deeply damaged by disease or ageing. From the outside, the body seems permanently marred, degraded and wrecked. To use Paul's word, the body has become 'dishonourable'. And yet, once you get to know the person, you can see that there is a beauty within. People are often more wonderful inside than their bodies reveal on the outside: there is a hidden glory. It is what the nurses noticed about the elderly Christian lady Ann, mentioned earlier: 'We all call her "the Angel Gabriel" because she shines!'

What Paul seems to promise is that our resurrection bodies will display that glory openly. But it will not be our own personal glory: it will be because we will all participate in the glory and light of Christ's body, in Christ's glorified humanity. The humiliated and dishonoured Jesus was raised, and (strikingly) his wounds were raised with him, dignified, exalted, glorified. The glory of Christ was revealed for a short period on the mountain of Transfiguration in the form of light such that the disciples could not bear to look at him. In some sense it seems that the same glory will indwell and transform our future bodies. Each embodied person raised in glory will be honoured because Christ's glory will shine through him or her.

C. S. Lewis wrote,

> It is a serious thing to live in a society of possible gods and goddesses, to remember that the dullest, most uninteresting

person you can talk to may one day be a creature which, if you saw it now, you would be strongly tempted to worship, or else a horror and a corruption such as you now meet, if at all, only in a nightmare. . . . There are no ordinary people. You have never talked to a mere mortal.[1]

'It is sown in weakness; it is raised in power' (1 Corinthians 15:43)

The dying person knows only too well the weakness of the fragile body. For many, as they approach the end, there is a sense of power and vitality ebbing away. Yet our risen bodies will be raised in the power of the Holy Spirit. It is the same power, the vitality, the dynamism, that raised Jesus from the dead.

In the life that is to come we will continue to depend upon the power of the Father, of Christ and of the Spirit – but the risen body will, by the grace of God, have powers to relate to others, to relate to the entire redeemed cosmos and to God himself. Our bodies are essential to our relationships. They are the means by which we relate to one another, the physical sign of our presence. To be embodied is to be in relationship, and that will remain the case with our resurrection bodies. God's plan for us in the new creation is not that we should float around as disembodied spirits; rather, it is for us to be embodied and therefore in continuing, profound and open relationships with one another. We are called to be in communion and in union with one another and with the persons of the Holy Trinity – in everlasting *shalom*.

The relationships that we have enjoyed in our natural bodies will (in some sense) continue in our resurrection bodies. In the Gospel narratives, the risen Christ appears to those he has known and loved beforehand, and he knows and loves them still. He knew Peter beforehand (including his failure and repeated betrayal before the cross), and he talks to Peter and offers him forgiveness and restoration afterwards. He knew Mary beforehand, and their profound and unique relationship continues after he is raised: 'Mary', 'Rabboni!' (John 20:16). Fellowship, forgiveness and caring were characteristics of his relationships to others before the resurrection, and they still are for the risen Christ. He loved to spend time with his disciples and to have fellowship meals with them before, and after the resurrection he cooks a barbecue for them on the shore of the Sea of Tiberias. He is still the same person – the same, but wonderfully different. And he promised his disciples at that strange and poignant last supper that he would drink wine with them again – at the coming banquet, the wedding feast of the Lamb.

In the new heaven and the new earth 'there will be . . . greeting and blessing, laughter and love, joy and peace'.

In the new heaven and the new earth 'there will be no sickness that needs healing, and no tears that need comforting. But there will be greeting and blessing, laughter and love, joy and peace,' as Allen Verhey puts it.[2] Our relationships with others will be healed and redeemed; there will be forgiveness and reconciliation.

'It is sown a natural body; it is raised a spiritual body' (1 Corinthians 15:44)

The Greek words that Paul uses in this verse are 'a *psychikon* body' and 'a *pneumatikon* body'. It is not that our first bodies are physical and our second bodies are spiritual; both bodies are physical. Instead, it seems that Paul is referring to a change in what gives life to our bodies. Our current *psychikon* body is given life by natural biological processes and chemical forces. But our resurrection body will in some sense be given life by the Holy Spirit of God – it will be a spiritually driven body, a *pneumatikon* body. The Spirit will fully indwell and transform our bodies; we will be completely 'filled with the Spirit'.

But this is a reality that is not totally confined to the future. The teaching of the New Testament suggests that we can have a glimpse, a foretaste, of the experience here and now. The more we allow the Holy Spirit to indwell our current bodies, minds and hearts, perhaps the more we get a taste of what it will mean to have a *pneumatikon* body. And as we approach the end of life, this foretaste becomes more meaningful and more precious.

Ruth van den Broek wrote,

> Those of us with respiratory problems are blessed to have permanent reminders of the importance of breath, connection with the Spirit, and the coming of our *pneumatikon* bodies – though I can't wait to be perfect and not need those reminders any more![3]

' "The first man Adam became a living being"; the last Adam became a life-giving spirit' (1 Corinthians 15:45)

The first Adam became a living being because the breath of life (in Hebrew *ruach*, 'spirit') was breathed into him in the Garden of Eden: 'the LORD God formed the man of dust from the ground and breathed into his nostrils the breath of life, and the man became a living creature' (Genesis 2:7). On Easter day Jesus was raised to life by the power of the Spirit. But now that life is flowing out from Christ through the power of the Spirit to bring other physical bodies to life also. The life of our risen bodies is continually held in being by the life-giving nature of Christ's risen body. As long as Christ lives at the right hand of the Father, our bodies will continue to live.

'Just as we have borne the image of the man of dust, we shall also bear the image of the man of heaven' (1 Corinthians 15:49)

Our current bodies bear the likeness of Adam's body made from dust: frail, vulnerable and open to chance events. But worse, our bodies bear the marks and the all-pervading contamination of the fall. They are vulnerable to disease, decay, pain and futility. Mysteriously, our bodies are subject to the terrible curses that the Creator pronounced in the Garden of Eden:

> By the sweat of your face
> you shall eat bread,
> till you return to the ground,
> for out of it you were taken;
> for you are dust
> and to dust you shall return.
> (Genesis 3:19)

But our bodies will be raised with a new likeness. As the apostle John put it, 'Beloved, we are God's children now, and what we will be has not yet appeared; but we know that when he appears we shall be like him, because we shall see him as he is' (1 John 3:2). We do not know in what form our future bodies will appear, but we know this much: our bodies will be like Christ's body – that body that walked on the Emmaus road and prepared breakfast on the shore of the lake. And how do we know this? asks the apostle. Because we shall see him as he really is. The glorious appearance of Christ will not be veiled or hidden from us. And that unimaginable sight, the glory of God in the face of Jesus Christ, is in itself life-giving and transformative.

Falling asleep

It is very striking that the New Testament rarely speaks of believers in Christ 'dying'. Time and again the phrase that is used is that of believers 'falling asleep'. In the 1 Corinthians 15 passage that we have been looking at, Paul uses the phrase three times: 'Then he appeared to more than five hundred brothers at one time, most of whom are still alive, though some have *fallen asleep*' (verse 6); 'if Christ has not been raised, your faith is futile and you are still in your sins. Then those also who have *fallen asleep in Christ* have perished' (verses 17–18); 'But in fact Christ has been raised from the dead, the firstfruits of those who have *fallen asleep*' (verse 20; all emphasis added).

In the first letter to the Thessalonians, Paul uses the same phrase three times in the same section: 'Brothers, we do not want you to be ignorant about those who *fall asleep*' (1 Thessalonians 4:13 NIV 1984); 'God will bring with Jesus those who have *fallen asleep* in him' (verse 14 NIV); '. . . will certainly not precede those who have *fallen asleep*' (verse 15 NIV; all emphasis added).

There is no doubt that this expression was commonly used in the early Christian church, and it is very likely that believers had learnt to use these words from the example of Jesus himself. To the funeral mourners at the house of the bereaved ruler Jesus said, 'The girl is not dead but *sleeping*' (Matthew

9:24), while following the death of Lazarus he said: 'Our friend Lazarus has *fallen asleep*, but I go to awaken him' (John 11:11; all emphasis added).

Perhaps the most remarkable use of this phrase is at the martyrdom of Stephen in Acts. At this violent and horrific death, as the boulders thrown by hate-filled zealots were crashing into Stephen's body, Luke writes that he called out, '"Lord Jesus, receive my spirit." And falling to his knees he cried out with a loud voice, "Lord, do not hold this sin against them." And when he had said this, *he fell asleep*' (Acts 7:59–60, emphasis added).

Is this just a pious euphemism, a gentle phrase intended to shield us from the brutal reality of death? I am convinced that the words 'falling asleep' reflect both profound theology and a deep truth about the experience of faithful dying for Christian believers.

From a theological point of view, Christian believers do not really die. That terrible enemy, death, has in a sense already been absorbed and destroyed by Christ. That is the meaning of those words that Jesus spoke to Martha: 'I am the resurrection and the life. Whoever believes in me, though he die, yet shall he live, and everyone who lives and believes in me shall never die. Do you believe this?' (John 11:25–26). In Christ, the sting, power and grip of death have been fatally weakened; life has triumphed over death.

So if, in New Testament thinking, Christians do not die but rather fall asleep, what is the crucial difference between these two realities? The obvious answer is that the person who is sleeping is in a state of unconsciousness, but that person is *still alive*. Throughout the period of sleep, however long the sleep lasts, the person is still there, intact and unharmed. But while the period of sleep continues, the person is inaccessible. It is not possible to have a meaningful relationship with a person while he or she is fast asleep. The person is alive, safe, intact – but unreachable.

Second, we all know that sleep is temporary. From a medical point of view, there is a crucial difference between the unconsciousness of natural sleep and the unconsciousness of coma. When people are in a deep coma, it is impossible to know whether they will recover, and if so, in what state. It is possible for people to remain in a coma for weeks or months, and for them to die without ever regaining consciousness. If, on the other hand, people do awake from a coma, they may be totally changed: their personalities may have been irreversibly altered by brain injury. But when people are sleeping naturally, we know that they are going to awake naturally, and when they do awake, *they are the same people*. They are in no way damaged or harmed by the period of sleep.

So there are wonderful and profound theological truths behind this biblical phrase. When we fall asleep in Christ, in some mysterious way we remain alive. He holds our very being, our personhood, intact and unharmed. Nothing can harm those who have 'fallen asleep in Christ'. Paul, writing to the Christians in Thessalonica, reminds us that not all will fall asleep in Christ, since some believers will be alive when Christ returns. But Paul is at pains to reassure the Thessalonian believers about those who fall asleep in Christ:

> Brothers, we do not want you to be ignorant about those who fall asleep, or to grieve like the rest of men, who have no hope. We believe that Jesus died and rose again and so we believe that God will bring with Jesus those who have fallen asleep in him.
> (1 Thessalonians 4:13–14 NIV 1984)

Paul is drawing an explicit distinction between Jesus *who died* and the Christian believers who *fall asleep*. Jesus experienced the full reality of death so that we might fall asleep. And the logic of the passage is that we do not need to grieve over those who have fallen asleep, because Jesus is going to wake them up again.

But, as I have reflected on these passages, I have become convinced that there is also an important psychological truth here. As they come to the end of their lives, it seems that many Christian believers are anxious and fearful about the process of dying. What will it feel like to die? Will I be struggling for breath, experiencing unbearable agony, overwhelmed with fear, sucked into a terrifying black hole of non-existence? It is easy for an overactive imagination to come up with all manner of horrors and nameless fears.

In response to these fears, it has struck me that, in his grace and compassion, our heavenly Father allows us to practise what it is like to die faithfully, to die as a believer and follower of Christ, every single night of our lives. You know precisely what it feels like to die in Christ: it is like falling asleep. I have tried to imagine that feeling of being exhausted and drained after a long and gruelling day, and then, at long last, your head touches that soft pillow. And all you have to do is to give way to sleep, because you know you are safe, secure and protected. Falling asleep is not something strange or terrifying; it is an experience that our heavenly Father gives us in advance so that we need not be fearful.

This reflects the ancient Christian tradition of using the period of preparation for sleep each evening as a way of preparing ourselves for death. This tradition reaches all the way back to the fourth century when Simeon's words in the *Nunc dimittis* were made a part of the liturgy of evening prayers in services variously called compline, vespers or evensong. We quoted earlier these words of Timothy O'Malley:

> As I prepare to sleep every night, I practice Simeon's own readiness to die as one who has encountered 'the light of the nations'.
>
> In this way, to pray the Nunc Dimittis is a counter-cultural performance in which each day the Christian practices the art of dying.[4]

To push the analogy a little further, the person who falls asleep in Christ is not only giving way to sleep after a long, gruelling and exhausting day, falling asleep in total safety and security, but falling asleep on the first night of the holidays, with all the anticipation, excitement and joy of waking up in the morning.

Awakening to behold the face of God

If the New Testament consistently talks about falling asleep in Christ, the Old Testament teaches us about awakening.

Isaiah sings triumphantly of the resurrection of the righteous from death:

> Your dead shall live; their bodies shall rise.
>> You who dwell in the dust, *awake* and sing for joy!
> (Isaiah 26:19, emphasis added)

But it is particularly in Psalm 17 that David links awakening from death with beholding the face of God:

> As for me, I shall behold your face in righteousness;
>> *when I awake*, I shall be satisfied with your likeness.
> (Psalm 17:15, emphasis added)

In Old Testament times, to see the face of the king meant being admitted into his presence. The supreme honour for Moses was that he had seen the face of the Lord:

> With him I speak face to face,
>> clearly and not in riddles;
>> he sees the form of the LORD.
>
> (Numbers 12:8 NIV)

David's psalms in particular express the hope of meeting God after death:

> Therefore my heart is glad and my tongue rejoices;
>> my body will also rest secure,
> because you will not abandon me to the realm of the dead,
>> nor will you let your faithful one see decay.
> You make known to me the path of life;
>> you will fill me with joy in your presence,
>> with eternal pleasures at your right hand.
>
> (Psalm 16:9–11 NIV)

> How precious to me are your thoughts, God!
>> How vast is the sum of them!
>
> . . .
>
>> when I awake, I am still with you.
>
> (Psalm 139:17–18 NIV)

The theme of seeing God face to face is continued in the New Testament. In the passage we noted above the apostle John says, 'we shall see him as he is' (1 John 3:2). Paul echoes the thought: 'Now we see only a reflection as in a mirror; *then we shall see face to face*. Now I know in part; then I shall know fully, even as I am fully known' (1 Corinthians 13:12 NIV). And it is spelled out clearly at the end of the book of Revelation, in the vision of the new Jerusalem: 'The throne of God and of the Lamb will be in the city, and his servants will serve him. *They will see his face*, and his name will be on their foreheads' (Revelation 22:3–4 NIV; all emphasis added).

There are deep mysteries about dying that we cannot penetrate. The reality is hidden from us in darkness and obscurity. It is still the valley of the shadow of death, and all of us are tempted to fear. But the Scriptures give us strong and unshakeable foundations on which we can rely. We fall asleep in Christ, we sleep in safety and security, and we awaken to see his face. We cannot know much about the experience of dying faithfully. But do we need to know any more, as we face the darkness at the ending of our own lives?

Living and dying in the light of the future

In Christian thinking, the wonderful new age – the era that was initiated by Christ's bodily resurrection and which reaches forward to the resurrection of the dead and the coming of the new heaven and the new earth – is already reaching backwards into our age. In a strange way, this current broken, marred and fallen age is being invaded from the future. The new way of being has already started, and our present lives are being touched by the melody of heaven; our Christian gatherings, our meals and our celebrations should already contain a foretaste of the new age. And even the hospital bed, the intensive care unit, the care home, the hospice – the place of disease, dementia, pain and dying – can be invaded by a breath, a

Even . . . the hospice can be invaded . . . by the life-giving Spirit of Christ.

word, a fragrance, a melody, from the new creation, by the life-giving Spirit of Christ.

But not only that, it seems that the transformation of our physical bodies is a central element in the transformation of the entire physical universe. Christ's risen body was the firstfruits, the foretaste, of what God the Father has in store for the cosmos. In God's grace and resurrection power, at the end of the age our own physical bodies will also be transformed in the same way that Christ's body was transformed.

And then, as those physical atoms are transformed into the new reality, it seems that the entire physical universe will also be transformed into the new creation. At the resurrection of the dead, Christ's risen body will draw the human bodies of the redeemed community out of the old space–time into a new reality, and after our bodies will come the rest of creation – trees, animals, planets, galaxies, made into the new creation, the Cosmos 2.0.

That is why Paul says in Romans that the creation 'waits in eager expectation for the children of God to be revealed' (Romans 8:19 NIV). It is only by our death and resurrection that the whole cosmos can be transformed. The creation is now 'groaning as in the pains of childbirth' (8:22 NIV). I sometimes think we should try to hear the groanings. Yes, the creation is stunningly beautiful, but all those mountains, trees, waters, stars and galaxies are groaning. They are saying, 'How long, how long? This is not the end of the story. There is something far more wonderful to come.' Only by the redemption of our physical bodies can the physical creation, of which they are part, be ultimately liberated.

In the Romans 8 passage there is a symphony of groaning. The creation is groaning, and we too are groaning, waiting for the redemption of our bodies: 'How long, Lord? How long?' And the Spirit himself is groaning within us, with words that cannot be expressed: 'How long?'

The first gleam of dawn

I close with one of my favourite verses in the entire Scriptures:

> The path of the righteous is like the first gleam of dawn,
>   shining ever brighter till the full light of day.
> (Proverbs 4:18 NIV 1984)

I once came across a photograph that illustrated this verse. A pair of rock climbers had toiled through the night to reach the summit of a desolate peak in Alaska. While they clung to the freezing rock, one of them took a photo of the distant blush of the coming dawn on the far horizon. It is an image I have reflected on many times since. The night seems interminable, hopeless, despairing, endless. But out there, on the horizon, those who have eyes to see can make out the first blush of dawn. The day is coming; slowly, imperceptibly, inexorably, the full light and glory of the everlasting day are coming! Here at the end of our lives on earth we are called to carry on walking in the darkness, yes – but it is darkness transformed by the first gleam of dawn.

Appendix 1

For carers and relatives: practical, medical and pastoral issues

We know that caring for a loved one at the end of life brings special challenges. This section focuses specifically on a number of practical matters for carers, although we cannot deal with them in depth here.

The 'Further reading' section at the back of the book lists resources and websites where you can obtain further information and support.

Starting the conversation

There is no easy way to embark on emotionally painful conversations. In my work as a paediatrician I was often called upon to break bad news to parents. I came to the conclusion that there was no 'good way' to do this. There are, however, some ways that are less bad than others. Above all, we need to be gentle, and to show that we care and are prepared to 'be there'.

Often we hold back from having the conversation because we do not want to cause unnecessary pain. Perhaps we are concerned that we may 'make things worse', or that we will 'say the wrong thing'. Or maybe we are worried about our own emotions – that in speaking we may be overwhelmed by our own grief – and we wish to shield our loved one from our pain. In reality, however, the other person nearly always finds it a relief to be able to talk about concerns that have been preoccupying him or her.

Of course, we do need to choose a good moment and an appropriate setting, and our words should be sensitive and gentle:

'This must be a difficult time for you. Would you like to talk about it?'

'Would it be all right if we talked about what's going to happen in the future?'

Our primary goal is to *listen*, not to come up with a list of our own thoughts and suggestions. We should not be afraid of or embarrassed by tears, but rather allow emotions to be expressed. Gareth Tuckwell, for many years the Medical Director of Burrswood Christian Hospital, said:

> When I first went to Burrswood, and people cried, I used to over-comfort them out of my own need. When they were crying, I might put a hand out and say, 'It's all right' and stem the flow. That isn't always helpful. We need to cry and sometimes tears are part of our healing. Count it as a privilege when people feel safe enough with you to cry.[1]

Important questions

The following are some questions that it is often very helpful to ask. I have grouped them into two main questions.

1. *As you look to the future, what are you most worried about?*
What are your greatest concerns?
The answer to this question can be surprising. Many people
carry hidden fears and anxieties that burden them, but which
cannot be expressed. Their response gives an insight to the
internal pain that they may be carrying.

In my companion book *Right to Die?* I tell the story of
Cicely Saunders, the extraordinary woman who pioneered
the modern palliative care movement, a new way of caring
for dying people that went round the world. One of her most
profound insights was that the person at the end of life
frequently had what she called 'total pain'. There was *physical
pain* caused by disease processes. But there was also mental
or *psychological pain*, anxiety about what each day might bring.
Often the fear of pain was as bad as the pain itself. There was
also despair and a sense of hopelessness at the recognition
that life was coming to an end.

Then there was *relational pain*, concerns about the effect
of the disease or infirmity on a spouse or a child. Perhaps
there was a broken relationship, and now death was coming
with no chance of reconciliation. And, finally, there was
spiritual pain, perhaps from feelings of unacknowledged
guilt from past events, or a sense of the meaninglessness of
existence.

Cicely realized that each form of pain had to be addressed
in order to maximize the well-being of the patient during the
critical hours and days as death approached. She discovered
that, if anxiety, loneliness and spiritual pain were recognized
and tackled, very often the physical pain was much easier to
control and alleviate.[2] Conversely, it is a common observa-
tion of palliative care doctors that, when physical pain does
not seem to lessen, despite the administration of powerful
medical treatments, it is highly likely that psychological,

relational and spiritual factors are involved and must be addressed.

As we sensitively explore these four areas – physical, psychological, relational and spiritual – we allow our loved ones to express their hidden concerns and worries. Of course, we frequently won't have easy solutions for the anxieties and concerns expressed. But by being there, by listening carefully and compassionately, we show that we care. In the words of an anonymous quotation that comes from the hospice movement: 'Suffering is not a question that demands an answer, it's not a problem that demands a solution; it's a mystery that demands a presence.'

As discussed in chapter 5, some people have a paralysing fear of uncontrollable pain. In reality, with good medical and nursing care, physical pain can be controlled very effectively and either completely abolished or at least greatly reduced to the level of discomfort. Talking to professionals in advance can provide reassurance. Just finding out about the range of treatments available can help to alleviate specific fears and anxieties.

Others are anxious about embarrassing problems such as incontinence, or needing to have personal nursing care which may seem demeaning and humiliating. Some are worried that they may be deliberately starved or dehydrated at the end of life by healthcare professionals. Others are concerned about the possibility of becoming confused, a loss of memory or dementia. Allowing our loved ones to express their fears in an honest and open manner is a way of showing compassion and being the hands of Jesus.

Advance Care Planning
The UK government has published a framework for Advance Care Planning for those approaching the end of life. The stated aim is

improving care for people nearing the end of life and enabling better planning and provision of care, to help them live well and die well in the place and the manner of their choosing. It enables people to discuss and record their future health and care wishes, and also to appoint someone as an advocate or surrogate, thus making the likelihood of these wishes being known and respected at the end of life.

The main goal of Advance Care Planning is to clarify people's wishes, needs and preferences, and to deliver care to meet these needs. (Further information is provided in the Notes section.[3])

In *Right to Die?* I discussed the legal framework for decision-making at the end of life, and various options which may assist the dying person to ensure that his or her wishes are respected, including Lasting Power of Attorney and Advance Decisions. (The relevant section is repeated in Appendix 3.) Other difficult topics may need to be discussed with health professionals, such as those mentioned in chapter 5. Should life-sustaining treatment be carried on right to the end, for example, or would it be better to stop all active medical treatments?

All too often, I have seen invasive medical treatments transform the last weeks of life from a time of peaceful preparation for death into a miserable, wretched experience. So we may be called to support the dying person in his or her wish to say 'no' to the possibilities of invasive treatment, and to help medical professionals understand that this comes from a desire to die well and faithfully.

The topic of a Do Not Attempt Cardiopulmonary Resuscitation (DNACPR) order is a frequent concern (which I have discussed on pp. 82–84). When it is clear that the medical condition is terminal, in my view it is nearly always appropriate for a DNACPR order to be agreed. However, agreement to the order may carry symbolic significance that is beyond its medical importance, and this needs to be recognized by relatives and health professionals. It is important not to let the DNACPR decision dominate the discussions with health professionals, as it is of minor significance compared with other issues about the care that will be provided in the final days and hours of life.

When discussions are needed with health professionals, it is extremely helpful if a relative or close friend can sit in on the conversation, to hear what is being said and, if necessary, to act as an advocate for the dying person, to ensure that his or her concerns and wishes are being heard. It is also valuable for the friend to hear what is said by the health professionals. It may be helpful to agree beforehand what questions need to be asked; having a written list of these may be helpful.

People often have specific and widely differing concerns about the care that they will receive when they are close to death. A commonly expressed one is that they may be neglected and abandoned as death approaches, and that hospital staff may covertly attempt to ensure that they die rapidly by withdrawing fluids and giving excessive doses of sedation. These understandable concerns have led some people to insist that they receive active medical treatment right up to the end of life, together with clinically assisted nutrition and hydration (that is, food and fluids given by a tube, usually directly into the stomach).

Others have the opposite worry: namely, that the doctors will attempt to keep them alive far too long, using painful and distressing invasive treatments, instead of allowing death to occur from natural causes. These understandable concerns have led people to insist that they do not receive life-sustaining or active medical treatment if it can bring no benefit, and that clinically assisted nutrition or hydration should not be given in the terminal phase.

We need to recognize that each person is different, and good end-of-life care must be highly sensitive and responsive to the wishes of the individual.

A written statement of wishes and values

In my view, there is a place for a formal statement of wishes and values, written in advance by the individual. According to the UK Mental Capacity Act, this written statement must be taken into account by health professionals, by legally appointed attorneys, and by any others who may have to determine the individual's best interests. Although the document is not legally binding, it can be extremely helpful for everyone involved.

There is no specific format for the statement and it can be worded in whatever way the individual desires. It would obviously be helpful for family members and close friends to be involved in discussions about the content, to minimize the possibility of uncertainty or disagreement. It is also important to keep any statement up to date and to make sure that copies are given to family members, the GP and other doctors and carers who may be involved. It is obviously essential that key people in the person's life are aware of the document. Another practical tip is to encourage the person in question to carry a card in his or her wallet or handbag directing others to the relevant document(s) in the event of an unforeseen accident or health issue.

In creating a statement of wishes and values, however, it is not possible to *demand* that specific treatments will be given. Medical teams are not obliged to start or continue medical treatments if they consider them to be against a patient's best interests, and this includes artificial hydration and nutrition.

However, if there are concerns that treatments may be withdrawn inappropriately – for instance, in the case of a person with chronic disabilities who worries that doctors might consider that his or her life is no longer worth living – it is possible to record these concerns as part of a statement of wishes.

A sample statement of wishes and values written for a Christian believer facing a life-limiting illness is provided in Appendix 4.

Fear of abandonment
One of the deepest fears for many dying people, although rarely verbalized, is the fear of abandonment. We all fear the prospect of facing death alone, unsupported, without human companionship. Even the Son of God in the Garden of Gethsemane asked his disciples to stay with him as he faced the ultimate darkness.

So we need to assure our loved ones that, whatever happens, we will be there for them. We will walk this road with them to the end.

In an earlier book I told the story of a little girl who is frightened by the darkness in her bedroom. She calls down the stairs to her mother:

> 'Mummy, Mummy, I'm scared. It's dark in here. I need someone to cuddle me.'
> 'I'm sorry, dear, both Mummy and Daddy are busy and can't come now. Just remember that God is with you. He will look after you.'
> Long pause.
> 'But Mummy, I need someone with skin on.'[4]

People who are dying need to feel God's love expressed in physical form. Because we are human beings, we need human contact. We need physical arms around us. We need to hear the sound of a human voice. This is the way that God made us. And the greatest privilege we can have as we care for those at the end of life is to be God's love 'with skin on'.

In preparing this book, as I talked to friends who had cared for a dying spouse or relative, several commented on how significant and precious they had found the simple acts of caring for their loved one – feeding, washing, holding a hand, reading, singing, laughing. For many of us, in our busy and goal-driven lives, there is little opportunity for these simple but profound tasks. Spending time with someone at the end of life gives us a chance to rediscover the importance of simple acts of care and compassion, of just 'being there'.

2. As you look to the future, what are your goals for this stage of your life? What are the trade-offs you are willing, and not willing, to make? What do you long might happen before you die, and how might we help you to achieve this?

Some of these issues are intensely practical: where would you like to spend the last days or weeks of your life? Would you like to be transferred to a palliative care ward or hospice, or would you prefer to spend your last days at home? Are you prepared to trade the more limited care that can be given at home, compared with being in hospital, for the benefits of staying in familiar surroundings? If it is your dream to stay alive to see your daughter's wedding, are you prepared to accept more invasive treatment that may cause you greater discomfort in the meantime? If you wish to refuse all medical treatment, are you prepared to accept that this will probably shorten your life by some days or weeks? If it is your dream to make a last visit to a much-loved place, are you prepared to accept that the travel may pose some additional risks to your life?

When children are called to make decisions about the care of older parents, safety and freedom from risk often predominate. Yet this leads to a strange paradox. 'We want autonomy for ourselves and safety for those we love,' writes Atul Gawande. 'Many of the things that we want for those we care about are things that we would adamantly oppose for ourselves, because they would infringe upon our sense of self.'[5]

As carers, we may need to admit that sometimes it is our own feelings and wishes that predominate. Perhaps, if we are honest, we wish our loved ones to be in a safe place not just in their interests, but also in order to suppress our own feelings of guilt, so that we can get on with our own lives. Instead, we may need to accept that our loved ones may make choices that seem to be risky – for instance, insisting on staying in their own homes, rather than being admitted to an institution.

It is important to understand that, when doctors predict how long a patient may live with or without different treatments, this is not at all an exact science. In my own thirty-plus years of clinical experience I have observed that experienced doctors have frequently been completely inaccurate when it comes to predicting life expectancy. In fact, there is good evidence to show that many doctors systematically overestimate life expectancy in terminally ill patients. In one study of 500 terminally ill patients, 63% of the doctors overestimated their patients' survival time, and the average estimated life expectancy was five times greater than what actually happened. So if a doctor estimates that a patient has six months to live, in reality there may be only one month or so.[6]

In view of this, it makes sense to plan ahead on the basis that there may be considerably less time than the doctor estimates. If there are unfulfilled dreams and plans, it is important that they be put into action as soon as possible.

As discussed in chapter 5, the concept of 'twin-track planning' is helpful. In other words, we make plans simultaneously for two different outcomes. On the one hand, we make some plans assuming that the disease will respond to treatment and that there are weeks or months ahead. At the same time, it is important to make other plans for palliative care in case there is a rapid deterioration and there are only days left.

It is particularly important to think ahead about how to address each of the four aspects of the person's care that we considered above: physical, psychological, relational and spiritual. Who will provide medical and nursing support? Who will take on the tasks of physical caring and providing psychological support? How can existing relationships with family and friends be strengthened? Who will provide pastoral support and spiritual care? It is helpful to ask if there are particular individuals from whom your loved one would like to receive support.

In chapter 5 I reproduced a diagram showing a framework of stages in the dying process (p. 77). It is helpful to distinguish palliative care, which may continue for many weeks, months and even years, from end-of-life or terminal care, the care given in the final stage(s) of life, a period usually covering a few hours up to a number of days. During this latter phase the person may be described medically as 'actively dying'.

The individual may be fully conscious or may move in and out of consciousness. Control of unpleasant symptoms is even more critical than previously, and the family may need a great deal of intensive support at this very difficult time. This kind of care is often delivered in a hospice or a patient's own home, where possible, with detailed attention to the needs of the whole person. Even if there are complex symptoms and disease complications, a fully equipped hospice is often preferable to hospital care. Palliative care physician Kathy Myers told me,

> If the patient was fit for transfer, we would move heaven and earth to get them to a hospice, which is the symptom equivalent of an intensive care unit. The rate of deterioration may give some guide to the future. If the person is deteriorating month by month, then there are likely to be months of life remaining. If the patient is deteriorating day by day, then there may only be days left.[7]

But, as we noted above, medical predictions are frequently inaccurate. It is not unusual for an individual who appears to have entered the last hours of life to reverse course and show some temporary improvement, sometimes for days, weeks or even longer. The truth is that there are no precise ways of telling accurately when a patient is in the last days of life, or how many those days may be.

Instead, those of us who are at the bedside are called to watch, to hold a hand, to care and to pray. The dying process challenges the comforting illusion that we are in control of our own lives. Walking with a dying person to the end reminds us forcefully that we are fragile, limited and dependent beings. But this experience of finding ourselves in a position of powerlessness and uncertainty is also an opportunity for learning new lessons. As Alan Toogood's daughter put it, 'I came away . . . with such a positive view of dying. God was in control the whole time. As you put your foot into the darkness, God puts a stepping stone there.'

Leaving a legacy of memories

Kathy Myers emphasizes the importance of helping the person in the final phase of life to leave a legacy of memories for relatives and loved ones: setting small positive goals that can be accomplished within the limitations of the energy available, and doing something each day that loved ones will be able to look back on with fondness. Kathy remembers,

> A lady I cared for recently could no longer go to Paris as she had hoped, but she really wanted to have a great Chinese meal. So her family arranged a fantastic takeaway that they enjoyed together with her around her bed. Other patients have watched films together or looked through holiday photos with their loved ones.

Caring for a relative or friend who does not share our faith
During my conversations with many people in preparation for writing this book, several raised the sometimes painful, sensitive and conflicted experience of caring for a loved one close to death who did not share their faith in Christ or had no desire to talk about spiritual issues. There may be a painful conflict between our wish to respect the dying person's integrity and beliefs, and our longing that he or she would discover the reality of forgiveness and hope in Christ.

I do not have any easy answers to this highly sensitive issue that so many people face. We have to confess the limitations of our own knowledge and perspective. It is not for us to judge other human beings and the secret thoughts of their hearts. 'Deathbed conversions' are not common, but they do occur in the twenty-first century, just as they occurred in the medieval period of the *Ars moriendi* manuscripts. That is why the dying thief on the cross has always played a significant part in Christian writing about death.

A poem by Katharine Tynan entitled 'The Great Mercy' contains a couplet describing a fatal fall from a horse:

> Betwixt the saddle and the ground
> Was Mercy sought and Mercy found.[8]

We do not know whether an individual will receive the grace and forgiveness that is offered by Christ. Our duty is to show love, respect and caring, however it is received. We must treat people in the light of who, by God's grace, they may become. We must not abuse the trust placed in us by pressurizing or trying to manipulate our loved ones. But we can tell them that we are praying for them and perhaps ask if they would like us to read a Bible passage or the words of a hymn. For many older people in our community, hymns and prayers remembered from their childhood have a special resonance, whatever their stated beliefs.

Saying goodbye
Fatigue and poor concentration are common in the last days and hours. It is not usually possible at this stage to sustain a long and detailed conversation. Levels of consciousness may fluctuate from minute to minute. But the sharing of final words can be of immense significance, both for our loved ones and for ourselves as we face our loss.

'I love you.' Many of us find it hard to verbalize our deepest thoughts and feelings with our loved ones. But sometimes all that is required is a gentle touch or the holding of a hand. And words from the heart are a precious gift that we should not withhold on the final journey.

'I am praying for you.' Many at the end of life find it difficult to pray for themselves. It brings them comfort to know that they are being held in the prayers of others in the valley of the shadow.

'Thank you for . . .' This may be an opportunity to thank a parent or relative for everything he or she has given.

'Please forgive me for . . .' Here is an opportunity for reconcili-ation and a restoration of relationships that have become

distorted and hurt, asking for forgiveness for words or actions that are on our conscience.

'I forgive you, and God forgives you through the death of Christ.' As we have seen, dying may bring spiritual conviction about past sins and fears about coming judgment. The formal confession of sin and claiming of biblical promises of forgiveness can bring consolation and relief. 'If we confess our sins, he is faithful and just to forgive us our sins and to cleanse us from all unrighteousness' (1 John 1:9).

'Is there anything you would like to say to me or to someone else?' We need to show that we take our loved ones' words seriously and will act on them.

'I will walk this road with you to the end.' For some, the greatest fear is of being abandoned and facing death alone. We can express with our words and with our actions that we will be there to the end, showing God's love 'with skin on'.

'We will meet again . . .' This is a reminder of the Christian hope: this is not the end of the story.

A prayer of commitment
For thousands of years, Aaron's words of blessing have been used as people approached death; as we say these words, we join ourselves with a faithful community that stretches through the ages, one that founds itself on the promises of a faithful God:

> The LORD bless you and keep you;
> the LORD make his face to shine upon you
>   and be gracious to you;
> the LORD lift up his countenance upon you
>   and give you peace.
> (Numbers 6:24–26)

Appendix 2

Prayers

Lighten our darkness, we beseech thee, O Lord;
and by thy great mercy defend us
    from all perils and dangers of this night;
for the love of thy only Son, our Saviour, Jesus Christ.
(Book of Common Prayer, 'The Collect for Aid against All Perils')

Sanctify, O Lord, the sickness of your servant N., that the sense
of *his* weakness may add strength to *his* faith and seriousness to
his repentance; and grant that *he* may live with you in everlasting
life; through Jesus Christ our Lord.
(Book of Common Prayer, 'For the Sanctification of Illness')

Save us, O Lord, while waking,
and guard us while sleeping,
that awake we may watch with Christ
and asleep may rest in peace.

Now, Lord, you let your servant go in peace:
your word has been fulfilled.

My own eyes have seen the salvation
which you have prepared in the sight of every people;

A light to reveal you to the nations
and the glory of your people Israel.

Glory to the Father and to the Son
and to the Holy Spirit;
as it was in the beginning is now
and shall be for ever. Amen.

Save us, O Lord, while waking,
and guard us while sleeping,
that awake we may watch with Christ
and asleep may rest in peace.
(From the Service of Compline, 'The Nunc Dimittis
[The Song of Simeon]')

Jesus, our risen Saviour and faithful Friend,
We are so grateful for the assurance that You will never
        forsake us
and have gone ahead to prepare a place in heaven.
Thank you for the remembrance of those we know who have
        died in the faith.
Comfort those nearing the end of their lives
and grant them Your peace and confidence in Your promises.
Amen.
(Celia Bowring)

Lord Jesus, you overpowered
the control that sickness had
by curing people of their illnesses.
Those who were disabled were freed to walk again.
You calmed the sea

and showed that you had control even over nature.
You rose to a new way of living and showed that
    not even death had power over you.
With your power in our lives, everything that
    happens to us can be turned to good.
And so I ask you this day
to help me to transform my difficulties and draw goodness
out of what is negative in my life, knowing that there is nothing
in life or in death
that can ever separate me
from your love. Amen.
(Nicholas Hutchinson)

Oh Lord, for those in pain we cry to thee,
Oh come and smite again thine enemy.

Give to thy servants skill to soothe and bless,
And to the tired and ill bring quietness.

And Lord to those who know life soon may cease,
Draw near that even so, they find thy peace.
(Amy Carmichael)

Father,
If the hour has come to make the break
help me not to cling even though it feels like death.
Give me the inward strength of my redeemer, Jesus Christ
to lay down this bit of life and let it go
so that I and others may be free
to take up whatever new and fuller life
you have prepared for us
now and hereafter.
Amen.
(John Taylor)

The Church of England has a formal service for use close to the time of death. The text is available from the Church of England website:

https://www.churchofengland.org/prayer-and-worship/ worship-texts-and-resources/common-worship/ death-and-dying/funeral.

Appendix 3

Current legal framework for end-of-life decisions

This section focuses on the current legal framework in England and Wales, although similar legislation is now in force in many jurisdictions.

The bedrock of current medical law is that all decisions about medical treatments must be taken in the patients' best interests, and if patients have legal capacity to decide on their own treatment, they must give their free and informed consent to all treatment. If a patient with capacity refuses treatment, the doctors must respect that refusal, even if it leads to the shortening of life. If the patient has capacity, the next of kin and other relatives have no legally binding right to be involved in treatment decisions, although, of course, the patient may wish them to be involved.

In England and Wales, the Mental Capacity Act governs the care that is provided to adults who lack capacity to make decisions on their own behalf. The fundamental principle is

This chapter is adapted from John Wyatt, *Right to Die? Euthanasia, Assisted Suicide and End-of-Life Care* (Inter-Varsity Press, 2015), pp. 141–147.

that all care must be provided in the individual's 'best interests' and in a way that causes the least restriction to that person's rights and freedom of action.

According to the Act, every adult is presumed to have capacity to make decisions on any matter unless it has been determined that a person lacks capacity. The law also recognizes that each person may have capacity to make some decisions but not others. In other words, you may have the legal capacity to make a relatively minor decision, but not one with serious and irreversible consequences. All reasonable steps must be taken to enable you to make your own decisions, including ensuring that the information is presented in a way that you can easily understand. With regard to the care of the dying patient, if the medical team conclude that the patient lacks capacity, it is their duty to make treatment decisions based on the best interests of that patient.

The Mental Capacity Act sets out the steps that should be taken to determine a person's best interests. These will include consideration of:

- the person's past and present wishes and feelings (and, in particular, any relevant written statement made when he or she had capacity);
- the beliefs and values that would be likely to influence the person's decision if he or she had capacity;
- any other factors that the person would be likely to consider.

In addition, the Act states that the doctors should take account of the views of relatives, of any person who was previously named for that purpose, of anyone engaged in caring for the person and of any named individual with a Lasting Power of Attorney (see below).

Many relatives believe that they have the legal right or duty to make medical decisions on behalf of the individual who is dying. However, this is not correct. If the dying person still has legal capacity, it is entirely up to him or her to what extent relatives and carers should be involved. If the person loses capacity, then, under the Mental Capacity Act, the legal responsibility for treatment decisions rests with the treating doctors (and particularly with the doctor who carries overall responsibility for the person's care; in hospital practice, this is a named consultant). However, the medical team do have a duty to consult the next of kin, and other relatives and carers, as part of the process laid down by the Act, in determining the best interests of the patient.

Under the Mental Capacity Act there are two main ways for a person to make preparations in advance to help with decision-making at the end of life, when he or she may have lost capacity.

Lasting Power of Attorney

The first option is to create a Health and Welfare Lasting Power of Attorney (LPA). This involves signing a formal document that appoints one or more named individuals to make decisions on your behalf, if and when you lose capacity. The LPA may be given to a spouse, a close adult relative, a close friend or a solicitor. If you appoint more than one attorney, they can be appointed either so that they must act together or so that they can act separately. You can also appoint replacements if the primary attorney(s) become(s) unable to act. The LPA only comes into force once you have lost capacity and the LPA has been registered with the Office of the Public Guardian (OPG).

Health and Welfare LPAs cover decisions including accommodation, care and all aspects of day-to-day living, as well as decisions on medical matters. If you wish, you can give your attorney(s) authority to grant or refuse consent to life-sustaining treatment on your behalf. The medical team will be legally bound to follow your attorneys' decisions. The attorneys have a legal responsibility to act in the person's best interests. Registration of an LPA with the Office of the Public Guardian takes about three months, and so advance planning is necessary. An LPA can be made, revoked or updated at any time, so long as you still have mental capacity to do so.

An 'Advance Decision to Refuse Treatment'

The alternative mechanism laid down in the Mental Capacity Act is a legally binding document called an Advance Decision to Refuse Treatment (ADRT). This is sometimes referred to as a 'living will'. It is an expression of the person's wishes about future treatment, or about some other aspect of his or her general health and welfare that may arise in the future.

The main value of an ADRT is to *refuse consent* to a particular treatment. It is not possible legally to demand any particular treatment, but it is possible to refuse consent in advance, including refusal of life-supporting treatment. If the Advance Decision relates to life-supporting treatment, it must be in writing and signed by the person in the presence of a witness who must also sign the document. There is no form of prescribed wording, but clearly the more precise it is, the better.

At some future time, if the person is admitted to hospital with a life-threatening illness, the medical team will need to decide whether the Advance Decision is valid. In particular, they will need to determine that the Advance Decision relates to the particular circumstances and treatment(s) being considered. They will also need to check that the person has not subsequently withdrawn the decision, and that he or she has not subsequently behaved in a way that is clearly inconsistent with it.

What are the advantages and disadvantages of the Lasting Power of Attorney and the Advance Decision?

The Advance Decision is much more straightforward to set up than an LPA, and there are fewer formalities involved. However, in reality, it may be much less useful than it initially appears. It is very hard to predict in advance the precise clinical circumstances that may occur months or years later, when you may be admitted to hospital in an incapacitated form. As a result, the Advance Decision may turn out to be invalid in practice, because it does not deal with the precise treatments or conditions that are being considered by doctors.

Alternatively, it might be argued by doctors or relatives that the person has changed his or her mind following the writing of the document. There is also the possibility that an Advance Decision has unforeseen consequences. For instance, an elderly person with a life-limiting condition might write an Advance Decision giving blanket refusal to any form of life-support treatment. However, this might mean that doctors would fail to give intensive treatment for an incidental treatable condition such as pneumonia, even though such treatment might give a good chance of prolonging a reasonably healthy survival by many months.

The LPA, by comparison, is legally more robust and covers a very wide range of possibilities. Your attorneys are given legal power to act on your behalf, including in circumstances that you had not imagined in advance, always provided that they act in what they believe are your best interests. This means they must take account of your past and present feelings and beliefs. As a result, it is very valuable to write a separate document that sets out your wishes, beliefs and values regarding medical treatment and care at the end of your life. This document stating your wishes can be updated as you see fit. (See Appendix 4 for a sample statement of wishes for a Christian believer.)

The LPA gives very wide legal powers to the attorney. It allows the attorney to ensure your wishes are carried out, but it may create a level of responsibility that some may see as burdensome. For instance, you may wish to nominate a spouse or grown-up son or daughter as your attorney. Months or years later, you might be admitted to hospital in an unconscious state and an acute life-threatening illness might be diagnosed. If it is covered under the wording of the LPA, your loved one carries strong legally binding powers to give consent to or to refuse life-sustaining treatment on your behalf. The doctors will almost certainly be bound to follow your attorney's decisions. This means that your loved one must carry responsibility for life-and-death decisions on your behalf, and must live with the consequences of those decisions for the rest of his or her life.

Sample statement of wishes and values for a Christian believer

I recognize that my current illness is unlikely to be cured and that it is likely to lead to my death. As a Christian believer, this is not something that I fear. I look forward to going to be with Jesus Christ, who has promised me eternal life through his death and resurrection. I know he will be with me to comfort and support me whatever the future holds.

I am grateful for the medical and nursing care I am receiving at this time of need. I would like to be actively involved in all decisions both about my care and about those individuals and agencies involved in my care.

Where it is possible, I wish to be consulted about all decisions relevant to my care and to participate in those decisions. However, if I should ever lose the ability to participate actively in decision-making, I would like the following principles to be respected when decisions need to be made:

- I would like to be kept as free from pain and other distressing symptoms as possible.

- I would like to retain the ability to communicate with family and friends, if at all possible, and not to be given treatment intended to reduce my level of consciousness unnecessarily.
- I would never want to receive any intervention or treatment designed to end my life, regardless of how my level of suffering may be perceived by others.
- *(Optional sentence)* In the case of an acute deterioration in my condition, I would like to receive active medical treatment that has a reasonable chance of prolonging my life and preserving function.
- *(Optional sentence)* I would wish to receive clinically assisted nutrition and/or hydration if these have a reasonable chance of prolonging my life or of alleviating my symptoms, and if they are not causing me evident distress.

If my condition is deteriorating irretrievably, and in the view of the medical and nursing teams looking after me there is no realistic hope of recovery, I would accept and welcome palliative treatment instead of further attempts at active medical management.

I would not want to cling on to life in this world because I have a living hope of life after death and of a wonderful future with my Lord Jesus Christ.

My life as part of a local church community is very important to me. I would not wish my church friends to be denied access to visiting me. In particular, I value ongoing spiritual and personal support from my church leaders and from other friends, including the following named individuals:

....

If I am ever unable to participate in decisions about my care, I wish the following named individuals to be actively involved in the decision-making process:

....

Signed ....

Witnessed ....

Date ....

(adapted from *Facing Serious Illness: Guidance for Christians towards the End of Life*, Christian Medical Fellowship, 2015)

Notes and references

Foreword

1. From Leo Tolstoy, *The Death of Ivan Ilyich* (Penguin Little Black Classics, 2016).
2. From Jean Paul Sartre, *Nausea* (Penguin Modern Classics, 2000).

1. Dying in the modern world

1. 'Fears Grow for Nelson Mandela': the headline and story were published on 25 June 2013 and can be found at https://www.news24.com/SouthAfrica/News/Fears-grow-for-Nelson-Mandela-20130625.
2. Details about historical trends in the place of death are taken from Phillipe Ariès, *The Hour of Our Death* (Knopf Doubleday, 1981).
3. The statistics are taken from the Public Health England website: http://www.endoflifecare-intelligence.org.uk/data_sources/place_of_death.
4. The quotation from Allen Verhey is from his book *The Christian Art of Dying: Learning from Jesus* (Eerdmans, 2011), ch. 2.
5. The quotation from Desmond Tutu is from *The Guardian*, 12 July 2014, https://www.theguardian.com/commentisfree/2014/jul/12/desmond-tutu-in-favour-of-assisted-dying.

6. The quotation from Stanley Hauerwas is from his book *Suffering Presence* (University of Notre Dame Press, 1986).

7. The study of the impact of terminal patients' religious beliefs is A. C. Phelps et al., 'Association between Religious Coping and Use of Intensive Life-Prolonging Care Near Death among Patients with Advanced Cancer', *JAMA* (2009), 301: 1140–1147.

8. The words of Terry Pratchett, now deceased, were taken from the Dignity in Dying website: https://www.dignityindying.org.uk/about-us/patrons.

9. The quotation from John Harris is from J. Harris, 'Consent and End of Life Decisions', *Journal of Medical Ethics* (2003), 29: 10–15.

10. Elisabeth Kübler-Ross, *On Death and Dying*, 40th anniversary edn (Routledge, 2009).

11. The quotation from *Death: The Final Stage of Growth* (Touchstone Books, 1986) is from the Foreword.

12. Allen Verhey's assessment of the death awareness movement is in his book *The Christian Art of Dying: Learning from Jesus* (Eerdmans, 2011), ch. 4.

13. Information about death cafés is taken from http://deathcafe.com.

14. Jon Underwood's words are from *The Independent*, 23 September 2015, https://www.independent.co.uk/news/weird-news/death-cafe-set-to-open-in-london-to-help-people-engage-with-dying-10513844.html.

15. The phrase is taken from a letter from C. S. Lewis in Sheldon Vanauken, *A Severe Mercy* (Harper, 1977).

2. The art of dying

1. Some of the historical information about the *Ars moriendi* texts in this and the following two chapters is taken from Allen D. Verhey, *The Christian Art of Dying: Learning from Jesus* (Eerdmans, 2011). Other sources are Christopher P. Vogt, *Patience, Compassion, Hope, and the Christian Art of Dying Well* (Rowman & Littlefield,

2004) and Rob Moll, *The Art of Dying: Living Fully into the Life to Come* (InterVarsity Press, 2010). Copies of the original text and images from *Ars moriendi* documents dated 1415 and 1450 can be seen at https://commons.wikimedia.org/wiki/Ars_moriendi. See also http://bav.bodleian.ox.ac.uk/news/ars-moriendi-the-art-of-dying.

3. The opportunities that dying well may bring

1. On the relationship between the medieval *ars moriendi* tradition and Stoicism see Allen D. Verhey, *The Christian Art of Dying: Learning from Jesus* (Eerdmans, 2011), ch. 7.
2. For more detail on the relationship between the Christian faith and the rise of modern medicine see John Wyatt, *Matters of Life and Death*, 2nd edn (Inter-Varsity Press, 2009), ch. 11.
3. The words of John Dunlop are from his book *Finishing Well to the Glory of God: Strategies from a Christian Physician* (Crossway, 2011).
4. The quotations from Rob Moll are from his book *The Art of Dying: Living Fully into the Life to Come* (InterVarsity Press, 2010).
5. The words of Don Carson are from his book *How Long, O Lord? Reflections on Suffering and Evil* (Baker Academic, 2006).
6. The quotation from Evelyn Miranda-Feliciano is taken from *Enjoy the Sunset: Living Fully, Ageing Well* (OMF Literature, 2006).
7. Katie Bryson's words are from P. H. R. Bryson and E. R. Bryson, *Dying Without Fear: Reflections from a Young Artist's Final Journey with Cancer* (Wonderfully Designed LLP, 2012).
8. Ruth van den Broek's blog is at https://ruthvdb.co.uk.
9. Ruth van den Broek's words are from a personal email.
10. Ira Byock's words are from her book *Dying Well: Peace and Possibilities at the End of Life* (Riverhead Books, 1997).
11. Extract taken from the song 'When Love Came Down' by Stuart Townend. Copyright © 2001 Thankyou Music (Adm. by Capitol CMG Publishing.com excl. UK and Europe,

admin. by Integrity Music, part of the David C. Cook family, songs@integritymusic.com).

12. The quotations from John Dunlop are from his book *Finishing Well to the Glory of God: Strategies from a Christian Physician* (Crossway, 2011).

13. Vigen Guroian's words are from his book *Life's Living toward Dying: A Theological and Medical-Ethical Study* (Eerdmans, 1996).

14. Diane Baird's and Richard Bewes's words are from John Wyatt, *Matters of Life and Death*, 2nd edn (Inter-Varsity Press, 2009), ch. 10.

15. Cicely Saunders' words are taken from an article she wrote entitled 'Care of the Dying: The Problem of Euthanasia', *Nursing Times* (1976), 72: 1003–1005.

16. Philippa's Taylor's words are from a personal email.

17. Jean Pierre de Caussade, *Abandonment to Divine Providence*, English trans. (Ignatius Press, 2011).

18. The words of Boethius are from an ancient prayer which can be found in many collections. See, for example, *Pocket Prayers*, compiled by Christopher Herbert (Church House Publishing, 1993).

4. The challenges of dying well

1. Images of original medieval woodcuts can be found at https://commons.wikimedia.org/wiki/Ars_moriendi.

2. Dietrich Bonhoeffer's poem 'Who Am I?' is taken from Dietrich Bonhoeffer's *Prison Poems*, ed. and trans. by Edwin Robertson (HarperCollins, 2005).

3. The quotations are from C. S. Lewis, *A Grief Observed* (Faber, 2012).

4. The quotation from Margaret Spufford is from her book *Celebration: A Story of Suffering and Joy* (Continuum, 1996).

5. The quotation from Andrew Drain is from *Code Red: A Young Christian Surgeon Finds Job Helps Him Face Death* (Christian Medical Fellowship, 2010).

6. Allen Verhey's words are from *The Christian Art of Dying: Learning from Jesus* (Eerdmans, 2011). The quotation from George MacDonald is from *Unspoken Sermons*, 'The Voice of Job'.

7. The quotation from John Dunlop is from his book *Finishing Well to the Glory of God: Strategies from a Christian Physician* (Crossway, 2011).

8. The quotation from the *Book of the Craft of Dying* is taken from William A. Clebsch and Charles R. Jaekle, *Pastoral Care in Historical Perspective* (Rowman & Littlefield, 1994), p. 182.

9. Further historical information on and a thoughtful assessment of William Cowper's life is in Dr Gaius Davies' book *Genius, Grief and Grace: A Doctor Looks at Suffering and Success* (Christian Focus, 2008).

10. G. K. Chesterton's words are from chapter 4 of his book *The Outline of Sanity*, vol. 5 of his *Collected Works* (Ignatius Press, 1987).

11. Bishop Ryle's words are taken from *Expository Thoughts on the Gospels*, *Luke*, chapter 23. I'm grateful to Bishop Timothy Dudley-Smith, who referred me to this quotation.

12. The poem 'I Believe in the Sun' is referred to in many sources about the Holocaust. See, for example, an essay by Brett Buckner, https://www.aarweb.org/sites/default/files/pdfs/Programs_Services/Journalism_Award_Winners/2006Buckner.pdf.

13. Cheryl Dikow's words are in her piece 'Graceful Dying: The Gift of Allowing Others to Care for You', https://catholicexchange.com/graceful-dying-the-gift-of-allowing-others-to-care-for-you.

14. Allen Verhey's words are from *The Christian Art of Dying: Learning from Jesus* (Eerdmans, 2011).

15. Mother Teresa's words are from *In the Heart of the World: Thoughts, Stories, and Prayers* (New World Library, 2010).

16. Screwtape's words are from C. S. Lewis, *The Screwtape Letters* (Collins, 2012), ch. 28.

17. The words of Timothy O'Malley are taken from a 2016 piece entitled 'Nunc Dimittis and the Art of Dying', http://sites. nd.edu/oblation/2016/02/02/nunc-dimittis-and-the-art-of-dying.

18. T. S. Eliot's poem 'A Song for Simeon' was written in 1928 and first published by Faber. It can be found in several Internet-based poetry collections.

19. John Dunlop's words are from his book *Finishing Well to the Glory of God: Strategies from a Christian Physician* (Crossway, 2011).

20. The quotations are from J. R. R. Tolkien, *Leaf by Niggle* (HarperCollins, 2016).

21. The quotation from Rob Moll is from *The Art of Dying: Living Fully into the Life to Come* (InterVarsity Press, 2010), p. 34.

22. John Dunlop is quoted in Rob Moll, *The Art of Dying: Living Fully into the Life to Come* (InterVarsity Press, 2010), p. 38.

23. Pablo Martinez's book *A Thorn in the Flesh: Finding Strength and Hope Amid Suffering* is published by Inter-Varsity Press (2007).

24. The quotation from Atul Gawande is taken from his book *Being Mortal: Medicine and What Matters in the End* (Profile Books, 2014).

25. The quotation 'When I think about it now, caring for Mom . . .' is taken from Rob Moll, *The Art of Dying: Living Fully into the Life to Come* (InterVarsity Press, 2010), p. 65.

26. The article by Gilbert Meilaender 'I Want to Burden My Loved Ones' was first published in *First Things* (October 1991) and was reproduced in March 2010 at https://www.firstthings.com/article/2010/03/i-want-to-burden-my-loved-ones.

27. Ira Byock's words are from the book *Dying Well: Peace and Possibilities at the End of Life* (Riverhead Books, 1997).

28. John Dunlop's words are from his book *Finishing Well to the Glory of God: Strategies from a Christian Physician* (Crossway, 2011).

29. William Vanstone's words are from his book *The Stature of Waiting* (Morehouse Publishing, 2006).

5. Communicating honestly

1. The diagram is taken from the Independent Review of the Liverpool Care Pathway, Crown Copyright 2013, and is reproduced with kind permission. The Review, which recommended that the Liverpool Care Pathway be abandoned, can be accessed at https://www.gov.uk/government/uploads/system/uploads/attachment_data/file/212450/Liverpool_Care_Pathway.pdf. I am grateful to Dr Kathy Myers, who pointed me to this diagram and provided helpful advice on palliative care.

2. A helpful review of the evidence that opioids in palliative care rarely hasten death is Susan Anderson, 'The Double Effect of Pain Medication: Separating Myth from Reality', *Journal of Palliative Medicine* (1998), 1:315–328. It is available at https://hospicecare.com/resources/ethical-issues/essays-and-articles-on-ethics-in-palliative-care/the-double-effect-of-pain-medication-separating-myth-from-reality.

3. Guidance for healthcare professionals on the use of DNACPR orders is provided at https://www.resus.org.uk/dnacpr/decisions-relating-to-cpr. Guidance on Advance Care Planning is available at http://www.goldstandardsframework.org.uk/advance-care-planning. Detailed information about the UK Mental Capacity Act 2005 is available at http://www.legislation.gov.uk/ukpga/2005/9/contents, and from the Code of Practice 2013 at https://www.gov.uk/government/publications/mental-capacity-act-code-of-practice. Information and guidance about Lasting Power of Attorney is available from the UK government website at https://www.gov.uk/power-of-attorney/overview. Information and guidance about Advance Decisions is available from an official NHS website at http://www.nwas.nhs.uk/media/281368/20013_adrt.pdf.

6. Learning from the example of Jesus

1. Katie Bryson's words are from P. H. R. Bryson and E. R. Bryson, *Dying Without Fear: Reflections from a Young Artist's Final Journey with Cancer* (Wonderfully Designed LLP, 2012).

2. John Stott's words are from John R. W. Stott, *The Cross of Christ* (Inter-Varsity Press, 2006).

3. A practical example of handing over responsibility is in the creation of a Lasting Power of Attorney, which is discussed in Appendix 3.

4. The words of David Webster are quoted by John R. W. Stott in *The Cross of Christ* (Inter-Varsity Press, 2006).

5. 'How great the pain of searing loss . . .' The quotation is from the hymn 'How Deep the Father's Love for Us' by Stuart Townend. Copyright © 1995 Thankyou Music (Adm. by Capitol CMG Publishing.com excl. UK and Europe, admin. by Integrity Music, part of the David C. Cook family, songs@integritymusic.com).

6. The words of Jürgen Moltmann are from *The Crucified God* (SCM, 2001).

7. The quotation from John Swinton is from his book *Raging With Compassion: Pastoral Responses to the Problem of Evil* (Eerdmans, 2007).

8. Allen Verhey's words are from his book *The Christian Art of Dying: Learning from Jesus* (Eerdmans, 2011).

9. Michael Mayne's book *Learning to Dance* is published by Darton, Longman & Todd (2001).

7. A sure and steadfast hope

1. The quotation from C. S. Lewis is from his essay 'The Weight of Glory', reprinted in C. S. Lewis, *The Weight of Glory: A Collection of Lewis's Most Moving Addresses* (Collins, 2013).

2. Allen Verhey's words are from his book *The Christian Art of Dying: Learning from Jesus* (Eerdmans, 2011).

3. Ruth van den Broek's words are from a personal letter.

4. The words of Timothy O'Malley are taken from a 2016 piece entitled 'Nunc Dimittis and the Art of Dying', http://sites. nd.edu/oblation/2016/02/02/nunc-dimittis-and-the-art-of-dying.

Appendix 1. For carers and relatives

1. The quotation from Gareth Tuckwell is from Philip Giddings, Martin Down, Elaine Sugden and Gareth Tuckwell, *Talking about Dying: Help in Facing Death and Dying* (Wilberforce Publications, 2017).

2. Information about the life and work of Cicely Saunders can be found in Shirley du Boulay's book *Cicely Saunders: The Founder of the Modern Hospice Movement*, updated, with additional chapters by Marianne Rankin (SPCK, 2007), and from the Cicely Saunders International website: https://cicelysaundersinternational.org/dame-cicely-saunders.

3. Detailed information and documents concerning Advance Care Planning are available at http://www.goldstandardsframework. org.uk/advance-care-planning. Detailed information about the UK Mental Capacity Act 2005 is available at http://www. legislation.gov.uk/ukpga/2005/9/contents, and from the Code of Practice 2013 at https://www.gov.uk/government/ publications/mental-capacity-act-code-of-practice. Information and guidance about Lasting Power of Attorney is available from the UK government website at https://www.gov.uk/power-of-attorney/overview. Information and guidance about Advance Decisions is available from an official NHS website: http:// www.nwas.nhs.uk/media/281368/20013_adrt.pdf. Guidance for healthcare professionals on the use of DNACPR orders is

provided at https://www.resus.org.uk/dnacpr/decisions-relating-to-cpr.

4. The story of the little girl who is afraid of the dark is taken from John Wyatt, *Matters of Life and Death*, 2nd edn (Inter-Varsity Press, 2009). I am grateful to Bishop Timothy Dudley-Smith, who referred me to an earlier version of this story in Helen Lee, *The Growing Years* (Falcon Books, 1963).

5. The quotation from Atul Gawande is taken from his book *Being Mortal: Medicine and What Matters in the End* (Profile Books, 2014).

6. The quoted study on estimation of life expectancy is N. A. Christakis and E. B. Lamont, 'Extent and Determinants of Error in Physicians' Prognoses in Terminally Ill Patients: Prospective Cohort Study', *Western Journal of Medicine* (2000), 172: 310–313.

7. The words of Dr Kathy Myers are taken from a personal email.

8. The poem 'The Great Mercy' by Katharine Tynan can be found at https://www.poemhunter.com/poem/the-great-mercy.

Further reading and resources

The Archbishops' Council (Church of England), *Grave Talk* (Church House Publishing, 2015)

Shirley du Boulay, *Cicely Saunders: The Founder of the Modern Hospice Movement*, updated, with additional chapters by Marianne Rankin (SPCK, 2007)

P. H. R. Bryson and E. R. Bryson, *Dying Without Fear: Reflections from a Young Artist's Final Journey with Cancer* (Wonderfully Designed LLP, 2012)

Christian Medical Fellowship and Lawyers' Christian Fellowship, *Facing Serious Illness: Guidance for Christians towards the End of Life* (CMF, 2015)

Andrew J. Drain, *Code Red: A Young Christian Surgeon Finds Job Helps Him Face Death* (Christian Medical Fellowship, 2010)

John Dunlop, *Finishing Well to the Glory of God: Strategies from a Christian Physician* (Crossway, 2011)

Philip Giddings, Martin Down, Elaine Sugden and Gareth Tuckwell, *Talking about Dying: Help in Facing Death and Dying* (Wilberforce Publications, 2017)

Janet Goodall, *Children and Grieving* (Scripture Union, 1995)

Pablo Martinez, *A Thorn in the Flesh: Finding Strength and Hope Amid Suffering* (Inter-Varsity Press, 2007)

Pablo Martinez and Ali Hull, *Tracing the Rainbow: Walking Through Loss and Bereavement* (Authentic, 2004)

Rob Moll, *The Art of Dying: Living Fully into the Life to Come* (InterVarsity Press, 2010)

John Piper, *Lessons from a Hospital Bed* (Inter-Varsity Press, 2016)

Cicely Saunders, *Beyond the Horizon: A Search for Meaning in Suffering* (Darton, Longman & Todd, 1990)

W. H. Vanstone, *The Stature of Waiting* (Morehouse Publishing, 2006)

Allen Verhey, *The Christian Art of Dying: Learning from Jesus* (Eerdmans, 2011)

John Wyatt, *Finishing Line*, DVD and booklet discussions for church groups (CARE/Keswick Ministries, 2015)

John Wyatt, *Matters of Life and Death*, 2nd edn (Inter-Varsity Press, 2009)

John Wyatt, *Right to Die? Euthanasia, Assisted Suicide and End-of-Life Care* (Inter-Varsity Press, 2015)

Organizations and websites

The Art of Dying Well – Catholic Church website: http://www.artofdyingwell.org

Citizens Advice Bureau: https://www.citizensadvice.org.uk

Dying Matters – a secular organization that aims to help people talk more openly about dying, death and bereavement, and to make plans for the end of life: https://www.dyingmatters.org/overview/about-us

Hospice UK – information about independent hospices in the UK: https://www.hospiceuk.org

Lasting Power of Attorney – UK government website: https://www.gov.uk/power-of-attorney

Making a Will – UK government website: https://www.gov.uk/make-will

National Council for Palliative Care – the umbrella charity for all those involved in palliative, end-of-life and hospice care in England, Wales and Northern Ireland: http://www.ncpc.org.uk

NHS information on Advance Decision to refuse treatment: https://www.nhs.uk/Planners/end-of-life-care/Pages/advance-decision-to-refuse-treatment.aspx